Injustice for All Ages

By Thomas Wood

My Favorite Quote of All Time:

"Imagination is more important than knowledge."

Albert Einstein

I would like to add to this quote:

"Imagination is more important than knowledge," but knowledge of injustice can spark the imagination for revolutionary change.

Here are some more famous quotes that are relevant to my book:

"All tyranny needs to gain a foothold is for people of good conscience to remain silent."
Thomas Jefferson

"All, too, will bear in mind this sacred principle, that though the will of the majority is in all cases to prevail, that will to be rightful must be reasonable; that the minority possess their equal rights, which equal law must protect, and to violate would be oppression."
Thomas Jefferson

"Every government degenerates when trusted to the rulers of the people alone. The people themselves are its only safe depositories."
Thomas Jefferson

"Experience demands that man is the only animal which devours his own kind, for I can apply no milder term to the general prey of the rich on the poor."
Thomas Jefferson

"I like the dreams of the future better than the history of the past."
Thomas Jefferson

"For the love of money is the root of all evil: which while some coveted after, they have erred from the faith, and pierced themselves through with many sorrows."

(1 Timothy 6:10) KJV(The King James Bible)

Dedication:

I first and foremost dedicate this book to my beautiful daughters. They did nothing wrong and had to suffer at the hands of legality. When they grow up, I want them to be proud of who they are and be proud to be from a rare breed of human kind. Their father is simply a humanitarian and revolutionary to help others like them from having to suffer at the hands of the legal system.

I love you two more than anything in the world and want you to live your lives knowing that I am truly not a child abuser as the government has labeled me. I am a victim of the system.

To my oldest: I raised you since your birth. After you were born and I cut your umbilical cord, I held you in the NICU for an hour all to myself. That was one of the most precious hours of my life.

Don't let the world convince you that I am evil because I am not.

I also want to send a big thanks to the music industry for putting out real music that has captured feelings we all go through and expressing it in a way that we can feel it. This book couldn't have been written the way it was without your music. What I'm saying is during the writing of many chapters I had music playing in the background and I wrote as it flowed through my body. This book in a sense is a musical work of art; if you don't get what I'm saying it's ok. Some people don't get music.

Forward:

Before I get into the "Forward," I want to say that I have a director's cut that I will only disclose to the public if I no longer need to rely on an employer. It is by far, one of the heaviest, dark and badass books known to man.

Why am I writing this book? Why would you want to read it? Who am I to say anything about injustice? This book is being written because I simply have to write it. I can't stand living my life without sharing my deep sentiments about the injustices as I see them. What injustices you ask? Read it and find out.

Do I have the qualifications to write this book? Oh yes. If there is such a thing as street credibility, I have it. I will tell you things that will blow your mind that I have witnessed and experienced first hand. I will however not fully disclose all the drug related crimes I committed since it would take volumes—although I personally don't believe they are crimes (I believe any person has the right to do anything he or she wants if it only hurts his or herself).

I have lived through the extreme thoughts of physically fighting people--no one listens otherwise (except I would have only physically fought the people that committed the legal acts on me and my family). I would have then been convicted. I honestly at the time felt that it needed to be done for the good of humanity.

So why didn't I do it? I have attempted suicide on multiple occasions. So why wasn't I successful? I also felt driven to rebel against our inhumane laws. Believe me, I rebelled like you could only imagine. I felt the need to do that because the legal system as I see it, destroyed my life and I wanted to do exactly the opposite of what they wanted me to do.

So where did I come from? I was born into a middle-class family with one of the greatest moms in the world. I did not include my father as he worked all the time during my childhood. So what happened to me? Why did I fall and lose virtually just about everything? Do I just make excuses because I am really just a loser drug addict, as many will say?

I am writing this book to tell you my side. I never did follow through with my fantasies, but I am giving you the opportunity to try to understand the psychology of someone who had thoughts and fantasies of physically attacking people who I felt had wrongfully hurt me.

Why do I call this book "Injustice for All Ages?" My favorite drug counselor.... gave me the idea when I expressed my feelings to her and told her I was going to write a book. I loved her suggestion! This book shows how right and wrong are only illusions that are programmed inside your brain by the legal system. For example, what was considered right during America 's period of slavery is now considered wrong. Can you believe that during that time it was okay to own a black person and that they were considered less than real people? I truly get what fuels Reverend Al Sharpton and Jessie Jackson.

I also believe in the butterfly effect. A butterfly flapping its wings can cause a tsunami on the other side of the planet--well not really, but close. If you think you can't make a difference, you can. You have no idea what effect one simple action you take will have on history. Look at Rosa Parks, a human being just like you and me. She simply decided during the Civil Rights era that she would not move to the back of the bus. Sure, people thought she was crazy at the time, because segregation was legal. However, her one action potentially was the spark that stopped segregation.

This book is very philosophical. It contemplates our existence on earth and what impact we as individual human beings have on our world. By writing this, I may not change a thing, but I may at the same time have an impact on a future leader that does. I can't take power over America and restructure it the way I feel it needs to be a utopian society with very limited injustice. All I can do is write this and hope to have a butterfly effect on American history. I am not having delusions of grandeur; everything I say has purpose and is very real.

My friend, who is the exact same age, was a zombie for Halloween. When asked why he chose that makeup he said, "It is a political statement." Out of the dozens of people in the room, I understood him perfectly. Everyone else had blank stares.

Am I crazy? Read the book and judge for yourself. I want to challenge you to a new way of thinking. I want you to open your eyes to what the legal system isn't telling you. Another belief I have is that the media brainwashes you into how they want you to think, feel and behave.

Thomas Jefferson once said, "Sometimes there is a need for a Revolution." I understand his statement. A grandfather, many greats back, was a Revolutionary War hero and actually knew him and was in tight and planned battles with George Washington. He is also buried with a couple Presidents;

the only reason I bring him up is that I have Revolutionary blood.

I would love more than anything to help change our laws. I don't think it will happen because the oppressive powers are too powerful. Also, I think the majority of society will not care how laws are treating the minority because it doesn't affect them. How can you have a legal change with that line of thinking?

Remember, I just want you to open your mind to possibilities different from what you are dictated by the present enacted laws. The media and legal system will lie to you, usually to protect their financial interests. Case in point, we toppled the government of Iraq and killed its leader because of WMD right? Wrong. I feel we simply needed the oil.

This leads us to the question of, "Why are terrorists so mad at us?" Let me ask you this, do you believe our media and government tells us the objective truth? I certainly don't. I am not justifying what terrorists do, but their belief is so strong they are willing to die for it.

I can go on and on about looking at the other guy's side, but remember this is just the "Forward." I am ready to get this show on the road and begin chapter one. I encourage you have the courage to open your mind to a different and more enlightened way of thinking. I will *not* lie to you.

I know that what I have to say may sound scary, but it is very real. This book is my mark on the world. I am a futuristic thinker. One day, maybe 50-500 years from now they may say, "He saw it coming." I actually feel like I am before my time and I am stuck in the present.

Table of Contents:

Chapter 1

Where Am I Coming From?

If you read the "Forward," you probably are curious to know what I did or what the legal system did to me that was unjust—I will slowly get to that.

I used to be an elementary school teacher for many years. I hold a Master's Degree in Education with an emphasis in Instructional Accommodations. I moved from California to South Carolina with my wife and daughter because it was a beautiful place to raise a family and homes were more affordable than in California. We bought our own house and I taught fourth grade for about three years here in South Carolina.

Let me first take you back to the birth of our first daughter. At 26 weeks my wife started labor. She was hospitalized flat on her back for 8 weeks. At 34 weeks our 4 pound 13 ounce daughter was born. My wife was told that we probably wouldn't be able to have any more kids. Our first daughter was everything to us. We would do anything for her, and still will—even though she will never be the same person after the legal system caused an upheaval in her life.

Also, I want to say that I never had a criminal record and was a model citizen. I cared about the children in my classroom and still care about them to this day. I encouraged them and possibly had a huge impact on the rest of their lives. I had a proven track record of taking children from "Below Basic" to where they were supposed to be and beyond. I believed in each and every one of my students.

That being said, my family and I were really happy out here. Things were going great! We were living the dream. Our daughter was an A student about to be accepted into the Magnet program.

We had tried and tried but having another child seemed hopeless. Then, one day I was out in our back yard gardening, when my wife walked up to me to show me something. Out of the complete blue sky, I saw the pregnancy test was positive and we were going to have another child. I can't even begin to tell you the amount of joy that filled my heart—seven years had gone by since the first one.

Okay. To be honest, I have put off finishing this chapter because it is probably the most painful chapter of my life. I wrote the "Forward," and the last chapter already, but this chapter is really the most draining and difficult to get through. Why you ask? It is simply this: It is the best and the worst chapter of this book. It is the part that recalls the pinnacle of the relationship with my wife and first daughter and leads to my downfall.

I recently watched a movie called "Solitary Man," starring Michael Douglas. That movie parallels my life in more ways than one. If you haven't seen it yet, definitely go out right now to Blockbuster, Red Box or wherever you rent movies and watch it. It could be you. Don't ever take the gifts in your life for granted because they may one day be gone.

Getting back to this chapter. My wife told me she was pregnant and I was probably the most excited I had ever been in my life. To make a long story short, I remember calling my parents, who at the time had only one grandkid. I actually called them from my classroom after school, which would soon cease to exist. They were ecstatic!

Our daughter was having a difficult time though. She was pretty much a straight A student, with exception of some B's. She was about to enter the Magnet program at the school where I taught. It truly was one of the most beautiful experiences watching her elementary years. What was she having a difficult time with you ask? It was simply hard for an only child to accept having a little sister who may take away the families' love for her. That by the way is a typical emotion for any child to experience.

We did everything we could to make her feel more than a part of the baby being born, but wait till the tragedy that will strike in "Chapter Two." I honestly can't write much more in this chapter--it is too hard on me emotionally. I told my friend about it and mentioned that it brought a tear to my eye. In complete disbelief because I have confided everything about my life to him, he said, "Really? Just one tear?" Don't take your friends for granted because a true friend is hard to come by. When tragedy strikes, you will truly find out who is your real friend and who isn't.

I have gone off on a few tangents, but that is simply my author's craft.   Getting back to the difficulty I am having with writing this chapter. It is reminiscent of a time when I had a tight-knit family and had no insecurities, fears or real problems whatsoever (everybody has problems, but nothing compares to what is next). It recalls a time of perfect emotional tranquility with the world and my family, as well as with the students I used to teach--I still love each and every one of them and look forward to seeing their accomplishments.

That time of my life is now a distant memory that will forever connect me to my first born, but tragedy is about to strike hard. There are people who have it worse than me, but it's about to get unbearably bad for the average person…

By the way, I recently met a fellow who is a retired writer for the "National Enquire" and a few other big publications. He also wrote a book that was published. I asked him for advice about how to get my book published and he pretty much told me that I don't have a chance. Did that stop me from writing my book? Nothing will stop me less than death. I feel that this book is that important. I truly believe that I have something to contribute to bettering humanity. This book isn't about me; I feel I am merely a sacrificial lamb.

This book also goes beyond me just being a sacrifice for the good of humanity. When I was ordered by the court to go to a certain amount of parenting and drug rehab classes, I gained an invaluable look at a different part of American life that I previously had misconceptions about. I honestly used to believe that when you had your children taken away you were a child abuser. Don't believe that for one second. Yes, some children being removed from their parent's home is a good thing. But what I honestly believe is that for the most part, it ruins lives—especially the child's.

Chapter 2

My Downfall:

Now I am going to speed you ahead to the part where the baby was born, but real quick because it is very painful for me. I was teaching my class and the principal had someone relieve me. My relief said that my wife's water broke and she is headed to the hospital. I went there right away.

Here is a good time to bring up another injustice. My wife should have had a natural birth. They pumped her up with so much of the epidural that she was fully dilated and the baby wouldn't come out. The Doctor decided that "in her professional opinion," we needed to do a C-section. What was that all about? Look at real statistics. You will find that C-sections have gone up drastically recently. It is my theory that hospitals give too much numbing medication making a C-section necessary. Why? The answer is simple: $$$$$$$$$$$

Getting back to the meat of the chapter. The Doctor ordered my wife to be tested for drugs without her consent or any awareness whatsoever. Many people will say, "Oh, she must have signed something. There are so many forms. Who knows?" The truth of the matter is I have a copy of the Dr.'s orders and she admittedly tests routinely without any type of positive program to help the woman. No informational flyers were given. It is done, in my opinion, to all new mothers without the consent of any of them.

I'm sure many will agree with her, but let me tell you something about that. I was using cocaine recreationally. My wife used to smoke marijuana but never had done this drug during her pregnancy. When I came home after doing some coke (away from home), I brought her some pot as a present for after the baby was born and after nursing. That was the biggest mistake of my life!

I slipped and told her I got her a gift and I would let her know when the time was right. Women sometimes can't stand it if they are aware of a future surprise and so she begged and begged for me to tell her what it was. After I got her to promise she wouldn't touch it until I gave the ok, she got it out of me. She then wanted to see it. I fully trusted her, but one night she messed up and she had a couple of tokes. It was a one-time incident toward the end of her pregnancy (She was completely clean otherwise.).

After the birth, she tested positive for marijuana and the baby tested negative. In fact, the Meconiom (babies stool) was the true test that went way back in the pregnancy—it was 100% clean. The department of social services then comes into the picture thinking they need to save the children from us recreational "users." This DSS guy tells me he is taking my kids and putting them into foster care unless I get tested. I happened to have done some recreational drugs. I took the test and was not told if I passed or failed.

What next? About a week later, I was at my school--I believe during an open house-- when I got a call from my mother-in-law who happened to be out here (South Carolina) from California. She said the cops and social services were at my home taking my children. I could hear my 8-year-old daughter screaming in the background.

That moment would forever change my entire families' life. Because of my actions (which had nothing to do with child abuse) and reaction (going insane and going for death): It would lead to the split-up of my otherwise happy marriage; it would lead to the loss of my career and almost the loss of my house; it would also lead to poverty and bankruptcy; moreover, it would make me a terribly damaged person forever. Previously, there was never a problem, but my reaction to that one moment in my life would lead to me losing everything. Have you ever heard of Post Traumatic Stress Disorder?

That is my point of view. What about my daughter who suffered the most? Do you know what kind of irreparable damage it has done to her for the rest of her life? Let me reiterate that she was almost a straight A student ready to be accepted into the Magnet program at the school where I taught. She immediately went to C's and D's when this first happened. At this point in my life it is about 9 months later and she got in a fight at school today—threatening to kill a girl. She then slapped her. I talked about the butterfly effect in the "Forward." DSS in my opinion tried to destroy her psychological well-being.

Then when she was allowed to go from foster care to my mother and my wife's mother who were out from California to be the foster parents, she was told her court appointed guardian was coming over to check on her well-being. She pointed to a chair and said, "When she is sitting down, I am going to murder her with this knife." She then proceeded to grab a pair of pointed scissors and pressed the tip against her neck. She then said, "I am going to kill myself right now. You kill yourself then and we can be in Heaven together daddy."

I ask you this? Who has done research on how removing children from their home affects the children? Who has done research on how it affects the parents? I know I can't change anything even if I were President of the United States because when it all boils down to it, he doesn't have enough power to make the changes that are really needed (but he can still attempt to convince Congress). All I can do is hope to start a movement to help this type of incident from occurring to future families. By the way, I don't want to be President. I will however be happy to help whoever is.

What needs to be done? There is too much to write about in this chapter. I will briefly go over my vision though. If the legal system has a problem with people using drugs and being parents at the same time, they need to pay to have the entire family move into a commune and move forward TOGETHER. Frankly though, I believe that recreational drug use is NOT child abuse. What equates to child abuse is the removal of children from their biological parents and putting them into the foster system.

So how do we fix it? This country actually has so many deep-rooted flaws that we really need to do a minor rehaul of the legal system. I truly love my country and love football, music, art…. We really have many positive aspects of our country that we need to keep.

However, I have the passion of a world leader waiting for the perfect time to make changes; on the other hand, if that time ever comes I would like to only be helping behind stage.   How long has it been since we had much needed change in our country? There was the end of slavery, the Civil Rights Movement, and women finally being able to vote, but our country is desperately in need of a minor overhaul. I can't stand it that I know what is needed and there is nothing I can do about it.

What kind of change would I make to DSS (Department of Social Services)? I thought about this very deeply. We could have been told. Arrangements could have been made for my parents to be guardians. However the ONLY reason a child should be taken from the biological parents is if actual child abuse is occurring. I will get into more detail later.

I would also make all drugs legal on reservations in each state. People are going to use drugs no matter what. The drug war is a joke! It only creates countless murders, crimes, and unbelievable debt that we spend fighting it. The problem with this country is that the TV is our God and we are programmed to be vindictive toward people who use drugs. I've known many drug dealers who have a wife and kids. They tend to have very stable and privileged lives, unlike what the propaganda tells us.

Look at the major news networks. Fox News programs the nation to be Republican. People say CNN is more Democrat friendly and less biased, but the masses are controlled through the media.

Getting back to my story, the DSS worker that came to my house was cracking jokes and laughing with the cops as my children were being literally pulled from their mother's arms. DSS has victimized my family very similar to the Jews by the Nazi's before and during World War II.

This brings up another point I want to make. How much can a human being tolerate before they snap? I certainly almost snapped and wanted to harm the DSS person that took my children. Taking someone's children is inhumane and cruel. It ruins everybody involved psychologically, especially the kids. What kind of potentially biased, selfish and vindictive party put together this outfit? Who ever it was probably had good intentions, but DSS is completely out of hand and they are simply causing more harm than good.

They very simply need significant downsizing, as a partial remedy for now. The ONLY reason children should be taken from the home is for actual abuse where there is clear evidence. What country do we live in when you are considered guilty of child abuse by a positive drug screen? Especially knowing that they are throwing children into foster care (a cruel and corrupt system).

I personally know parents from my parenting class that lost their precious child due to neglect in the foster home. I know a mom who had pictures on her cell phone of her brutally beaten son from foster care. I want to say that there are good foster parents out there, but I have personally seen the foster system used as a business.

Some foster parents see the kids as cogs in a money making machine. If children are being used to make 900 a head, costs are cut to squeeze the most possible profit. Sure, these particular foster parents buy a nice outfit to put on a show for the few and far between visits, but the foster care system I believe to be very abusive psychologically—even if the child has the best foster parents in the world. Again, who has done the research? I charge the people who put together DSS with neglect against the countless children that they place.

I also want to mention in this chapter that the foster care system needs to be completely eliminated and we need to have taxpayer financed family care units that improve lives rather then completely destroying them. The only reason I say "taxpayer financed" is that the taxpayers supposedly vote for the laws or at least vote for politicians that create the laws. If "We the People" have a problem, thinking that drug use is child abuse, we need to pay for it. I can tell you the real truth though. Drug use is NOT child abuse and you have all been programmed to view it that way.

I can go on and on about the crimes our legal system is doing against humanity, and how they control your thoughts and feelings through the TV, but I need to wrap up this chapter. This horrible injustice that was done to my family and me got me to a point where I was ready to harm people; it put me into a different state of mind.   I was at war, since an act of war was committed against me. Again, many would disagree because there are a lot of misconceptions out there and the masses don't know it but they are under mind control. All I ask is that my voice is heard. I have the right to have my own opinion that clashes with the system. I thank you for that. Plus, I did not follow through with any of my fantasies.

Chapter 3
The Salem Witch Trials:

Look at the title of my book, "Injustice for all Ages." That can be used in terms of injustice to adults and children (ages) or you can look at it as injustice throughout the ages of time. Around Halloween our kids may dress as a witch never even thinking once how at one point in history, people were tried and found guilty of witchcraft and sentenced to death—sometimes burned at the stake.

I can bring up countless other examples throughout the ages when injustices were committed against human rights. Who hurts the most though? The children.

Here is a rap I wrote that expresses how I truly feel:

Yo, get with it man,
It's time to take a stand,
You get your kids taken by DSS,
For just having a positive drug test,
What ever happened to our 4th Amendment right?
Unwarranted search and seizures of property and persons of any kind

What about cruel and unusual punishment?
What about this wack and corrupted foster system where babies die all the time?
But it's blamed on SIDS (sudden infant death syndrome),
Where were the foster parents at throughout the night when the baby cried?
Fast asleep dreaming about the $900 a month profit from an innocent human being

Don't get it twisted,

Some foster parents are really good,

But if I could,

I would have safe zones where all drugs are legal,

Who cares what people do if they don't hurt anyone but themselves?

People have the right to pure freedom within reason,

Recreational drug use is NOT child abuse

To the US government,

You will NEVER win the war on drugs,

You will NEVER stop the thugs,

Unless you use my ideas

If the President would act now,

The murder rate would plummet,

The crime rate too,

And all these suicidal young children,

Abused by the system…

They aren't victims of their parents,
In most cases…

They're victims of the system,
The system,
The system

As a final note to this chapter, have you ever asked yourself about the word "using?" When DSS took my kids and they were coming at me saying that my children were "being abused," I told the truth and said that I wasn't abusing them in any way whatsoever. This one lady says, "Why were you 'using' then?!" in somewhat of a hateful tone. I never thought about this word before but it hit me that the word "using" is intended to give people an ill feeling toward people who do drugs. It is kind of a vindictive term.

When you go to a bar, you drink alcohol. In that setting, people are having a good time and sometimes smoking cigarettes as well. Those people are just having a good time. When you do a drug recreationally you are "using." Some people say that you are a "user." A better way of this lady going about asking that question is, "Why did you do some cocaine then?" Even though I will never agree that I was a "child abuser" like the system dubbed me, and believe that although sometimes people who do drugs are involved in child abuse, I just think my suggestion is a more humanistic way of asking that question.

I just had to throw that in because I find it very interesting. I never really thought about that though, until I got caught and started feeling the onslaught of negativity thrown at me. Even though I take responsibility for my actions, I firmly believe that I am a victim because I never hurt anyone but myself and the legal system destroyed my career, my family and left me a broken man.

Another thing I'd like to add is that even though doing cocaine was fun, I was also self-medicating. Are you aware that children are prescribed a drug called

"Adderall," which is pretty much pure crystal-meth? That is at least what people tell me who are doing that drug for fun or self-medication purposes. Why is it that these children are "on medication," but someone who does drugs for fun or medicates themself is a "user?" This is part of what I am talking about when I say that the legal system programs people to be vindictive. Have you ever thought about that?

Chapter 4

Addiction is a Disease:

Since our childhood we are taught to be vindictive toward people who "use" drugs. The truth is that people who do drugs don't hurt anybody but themselves. The reasons my family is torn apart and broken are because of my reaction (temporary insanity and trying to die) to DSS policy and the psychological damage they caused to everyone. I couldn't keep it together, like many fathers, and families are being torn apart. Again, who has done the research on how the kidnapping of a father's children affects him?

I believe that DSS consists of master puppeteers that work toward breaking apart families. Sure they will put out false propaganda telling you "Every child deserves a good home," but don't buy into their lies. Make no mistake; a lot of them are vindictive and power hungry.

I am going to take away some of their power right now. First, there is a difference between recreational drug "use" and full-blown addiction. If a recreational drug "user" ever gets to that point, professionals treat their addiction as a disease. Since the disease can eventually kill the "user," it is like saying the person addicted to drugs is a cancer patient. We would never be vindictive toward a cancer patient right?

How does the legal system control our thoughts? I have had an awakening and I have realized that all governments control people's thoughts and feelings to a certain extent.

I had it all figured out myself. I was doing cocaine recreationally for 8 years. I was always debt free, had tons of stocks and a fairly decent retirement. When DSS committed their act of inhumanity against my family, I lost it psychologically. You could say that I am still very troubled and it is 9 months later. My wife did as was dictated by DSS and the court and was given full custody of the children; in fact, I don't have any parental rights. Because of my rage I did cocaine in massive amounts trying kill myself.

At first I was without a doubt suicidal. I tried to kill myself doing crack cocaine at about 10,000 dollars a time a couple times—this would be carried out in the form of binges that would last for weeks where I hardly slept. Sometimes it would only be 1, 2, 3 or $4,000, but I'm not going to get into numbers. It doesn't matter. The point is that it was massive amounts. I had episodes where I would start to fade out and I was so glad that the pain would soon be gone. However, it never ended for me. One binge led to the next and to the next after that until I spent probably 40,000 dollars on crack in a short period of time. It might have been a lot more or a little less, but I'm not going to get out my calculator.

I also tried to commit suicide one night after a huge crack binge by taking a bottle of prescription sleeping pills and going to sleep with a cord wrapped fairly tight around my neck. That obviously didn't work.

So why am I still here? The answer is two-fold. First and foremost I am here for my daughters who are now living in California with my parents and my wife's parents. Even though I don't have any parental rights, the legal system can't ever take away my daughters' love for their dad. The government is just going to have to live with that.

The other reason I am alive is to fight the Revolution to make the changes necessary to America. I absolutely love my country and that is why I need to do this. I am willing to sacrifice myself for the good of humanity. I'm not Jesus, I just see a lot of injustices and problems taking place in my country and caused by my country around the world, and I can't stand to sit on it. The children are what matter the most.

I know that I would be mocked and laughed at if I still smoked crack as one of the leaders of a movement, but that is not why I am giving it up. I am giving it up because it is completely out of control now with me. Recreational "use" is one thing, but full-blown addiction is a disease and at this point, I need to heal.

Real quick, I just want to talk about Adolf Hitler. He tried to take control of the world and he was using crystal-meth injections, along with many other Nazis. There was nothing funny about Hitler.

We are trained to be vindictive toward people who "use" drugs. Another good example is the rock-n-roll bands of the eighties were worshiped for their drug "use" lifestyle. It was glamorized back then. Just remember, propaganda has the power to control your feelings. You are not really in control of how you feel about certain things, the government is.

As an ending note to this chapter, I want to put some advice in here for those who are suffering with an addiction. It will only work if you truly want to stop "using." What is the point that our addiction controls us? It is when our euphoric recall turns into a feeling. What I mean by that is that a recalled memory about last doing drugs starts in the brain. If you don't redirect your thoughts immediately, you start thinking more about that memory. Eventually those thoughts turn into trying to remember what it felt like. That then turns into a craving. Also, if you are addicted to cocaine, don't think you can handle a little taste because that small sample can throw you into a binge and you can go through your money in the snap of a finger.

Chapter 5

I Am a Vampire:

It started when I worked a graveyard shift at a restaurant about 8 or 9 years ago. Cocaine was rampant and multiple lines were put before me on a regular basis. I actually did drugs before at college and soon after my high school years, however I want to focus on how I turned into a vampire—you will see what I mean by "vampire" in a minute.

So, about 8 or 9 years ago, I started to do coke recreationally. I was NOT a vampire at that point. What do vampires need? Right! They roam around at night hunting for blood. The day DSS took my children is the day I turned into a vampire, however I didn't lose control until my career ended. Before that one moment in time (the kidnapping), I was pretty much a model citizen (the butterfly effect). Had that moment never happened, I would be still be helping children learn and serving my own children as a great dad.

When you are a vampire, the world (at the time of writing this book) wants to drive a wooden stake in your heart. I put "at the time of writing this book," because of the butterfly effect. What if writing this one book has a major effect on people's attitudes toward people who do drugs?

Again, I want to reiterate what Rosa Parks did for humanity because she alone is the BEST example in the world to help people understand the butterfly effect. She was an ordinary human being like myself. At her time in history, she was thought to be crazy by not getting up out of her seat. What butterfly effect did she have on the Civil Rights Movement? What if she decided she would give up her seat after all? The future is uncertain and one simple action by any human being in this world can create massive world change.

My Vampire Poem: (Blood is used to show desire for crack or cocaine.)

A vampire once bit me,
I am one now,
I thirst for fresh blood,
I try to fight my raw and primeval urges,
I want to feast on a sexy virgin's blood,
My urges are tied deep to my sexuality,
emotions and carnal instincts,
It feels like I need blood to survive,
But I don't really,
I am a good vampire and I can live without blood,
But it is so, so hard,
It is almost beyond my choice,
But I can live without blood…

When I am tempted with a virgin I start to
breath heavy,
My teeth become sharp,
I want to bite her neck and feel pure ecstasy,
I love my private heaven,
But the world hates vampires,
I must fight my urges,
I must remain a good vampire…

Please don't tempt me,
For I am a vampire,
Please don't hate me,
For I am a vampire like someone is stuck
with a disease,
I am a vampire and forever will be…

I am now a vampire till my death,
Give me refuge,
Don't be vindictive,
Help me….
I need it

Raw and true,

I roam the shadows between life and death,

I am a vampire

Chapter 6

What Needs to Be Done with the Department of Social Services:

First and foremost, everybody from the Department of Social Services needs to be phased out and have their jobs eliminated. I know that there are good people in this department and we don't need to seek justice on everybody. However, I don't want any old way of doing business to taint an otherwise pure and good-natured organization.

After everyone is gone, we need to reinvent the organization, but on a significantly smaller scale. What has happened is that too many people work for this department and some are not good at their jobs, some don't care and many act out vindictively.

I have very real street credit. I am deeply connected to what some call "the hood." I know many dealers and people who do drugs and I personally taught their children— so I have a unique perspective. The majority of these children have happy lives and they are NOT being abused. The major abuse that is occurring is when the children get taken away from their happy families and get thrown into a corrupt and unstable foster care system (business).

In the name of the children, we need to ONLY protect the ones that are truly being abused. There was once a point in our nation when we were presumed innocent until proven guilty. Isn't that the way it's supposed to be? Not anymore!

We are losing more and more of our Constitutional Rights every day. If we don't have a change now, one day, we will all have microchips implanted in our bodies. If we try to remove them, we will be injected with poison. All our cars will be tracked and filmed by satellites. We will also ALL have cameras in every room of our house.

Make no mistake; the future is very dark and bleak for humans unless we enact change now. I encourage all Americans to take a stand against this governmental beast that is causing more harm than good. Again, don't misunderstand me; I love my country and want to keep most of what it represents—our founding fathers were geniuses. However, a time in history has come where we need to do a restructuring of our government. We are becoming a nation of "We know what's best for everybody."

We need to keep our Constitution and we don't need to burn down the White House.

We simply need to act for what is best for the good of humanity.

Chapter 7

New Privacy Law Enactments:

In South Carolina, where I live, there is an entertainment newspaper that profits from public humiliation. In particular, there is a game called "Guess the Perp" where mug shots of child molesters are juxtaposed with people who possessed drugs and with rapists. The buyer of the newspaper gets to try to figure out who committed what crime.

I never had a record, but when I lost my children I went insane. At one point, I got pulled over for drinking and driving. The truth about that is that I had a couple beers and was profiled from the club when I was driving home. Yes, I had time to sober up, but the officer claims I was "swerving and weaving all over the road."

I was taken to the "Detention Center" and locked up. The entire time in custody, I was going off about DSS and the fact that I no longer have the will to live. I also thanked the cop for giving me some more "street cred." When it came time for the Breathalyzer, I told the cop, "You can take your Breathalyzer and shove it up your A@$#%."

It's all on the video that I possess as evidence for my jury trial. The interesting thing is that the part where I was apparently "swerving and weaving" is completely cut out of the video. Why would they do that if they were completely unbiased? The answer is simple: They want to convict me.

When it was my turn to take my picture for the South Carolina perp paper, I flipped off the camera and smiled. I said, "Here's my mug shot bit@#$es!" However, since I was glamorizing my supposed crime, the people in charge started yelling at me and finally convinced me to take down my finger.

When placed in the cell, they then proceeded to freeze me by cranking on the AC and refusing to give me a blanket. In fact, they teased me with one placed right outside my cell. I then proceeded to mummify myself with toilet paper.

I was literally shivering when the copper entered my cell and proceeded to yell at me that I was "wasting taxpayer dollars!" I simply asked for my blanket. They never gave it to me.

Again, I will go off on tangents that detail other injustices whenever I can, but the point of this chapter is on public humiliation. Do you know how many drug dealers have personally asked me if I could get them a job where I was working? You can imagine that after being publicly humiliated (in a vindictive fashion) before the eyes of society, their chance of finding a job significantly diminished.

Moreover, when you apply for a job, your prospective employer regularly does ask if you have a criminal record. Since this information is public, when the potential employer does a background check, they will typically say they don't discriminate and then not hire you for another reason. Everybody messes up and we all deserve a second chance, but some people are forced into a life of drugs and crime. In a sense, the government is increasing crime as a result.

A friend has the opinion that my argument has holes because people can always "rake yards or create their own work." I welcome every argument and opinion out there, but who is connected to the hood and who isn't? I know how it really is because I have the street credit that goes with me wherever I go.

What is street credit? It is whenever you truly know what you are talking about because you have the real-life experiences that got you there.

What we need to do—the right thing to do—is STOP any public humiliation. Public humiliation by authority is a violation against human rights. In addition, ALL information of our criminal mistakes needs to be completely private. We served our time; we received our punishment. Why are you going to try to push us into poverty? The answer is simple: vindictiveness.

However, I do believe that if it is proved that you molested a child, people do have the

right to know. There are exceptions to the
rule.

Chapter 8

Let's Officially Mark an End to Hunger and Homelessness in Our Country:

Let's roll the clock back to when we stormed the beaches of Normandy during WW2. Thousands and thousands of those soldiers were drafted. When their country needed them, they were there to lay down their lives. Why is it that when our country needs us to spill our blood on foreign land we are willing, but when we are down and out we get our faces kicked in?

Talk to a homeless person. While others are vindictive, be the better person and find out his or her story. Some tried and tried and got turned down for work because of their criminal record. Some are just down and out. The key point though is why are we allowing hunger and homelessness in our country?

As one of the founders of the new order (I say only one of the founders because no man is an island), I would like to make sure that there isn't one person in our nation that goes hungry or homeless.

I believe in capitalism and a free-market economy, but how is it that the oil companies make billions and the money is used greedily? We need to target the corporations that make the most profit and tax them to fund programs that help our family—our nation.

As one of the leaders of our next society, I would encourage the government to treat each and every citizen as family.

Chapter 9

What Would Jesus Do?

In your heart of hearts, do you believe that Jesus would have enslaved black people? Do you believe he would have then segregated them? Do you believe that he would have approved of us lying about WMD? Lastly, do you believe that he would say that it is ok to rip a child from his or her mother's arms because the powers that be made a judgment that the parent is a "child abuser" based on a positive drug screen?

It's not just about drugs. Many, many, many parents lose their children for various reasons (i.e., the electric is not wired right, the back yard is considered too messy, someone makes a vindictive phone call....). Would Jesus say that our legal system is right to judge and act cruel and inhumanely based on someone's opinion?

These incidents are very real, but most people don't know about them because DSS tends to act against people of poverty. I happened to be educated and at the time I was a member of the middle-class (now I am in poverty too). I believe this happened to me so I could give the victims a voice. I am their voice. I will always take their side, unless there is undeniable evidence beyond a reasonable doubt that they are committing acts of real abuse against their children.

Chapter 10

"Universal Declaration of Human Rights":

I don't even need to say anything in this chapter, but I can't help myself. All I ask is that you please read the following and judge for yourself (all the following information is quoted directly from www.un.org, the official United Nations website):

"On December 10, 1948 the General Assembly of the United Nations adopted and proclaimed the Universal Declaration of Human Rights the full text of which appears in the following pages. Following this historic act the Assembly called upon all Member countries to publicize the text of the Declaration and "to cause it to be disseminated, displayed, read and expounded principally in schools and other educational institutions, without distinction based on the political status of countries or territories."

Universal Declaration of Human Rights

PREAMBLE

Whereas recognition of the inherent dignity and of the equal and inalienable rights of all members of the human family is the foundation of freedom, justice and peace in the world,

Whereas disregard and contempt for human rights have resulted in barbarous acts, which have outraged the conscience of mankind, and the advent of a world in which human beings shall enjoy freedom of speech and belief and freedom from fear and want has been proclaimed as the highest aspiration of the common people,

Whereas it is essential, if man is not to be compelled to have recourse, as a last resort, to rebellion against tyranny and oppression, that human rights should be protected by the rule of law,

Whereas it is essential to promote the development of friendly relations between nations,

Whereas the peoples of the United Nations have in the Charter reaffirmed their faith in fundamental human rights, in the dignity and worth of the human person and in the equal rights of men and women and have determined to promote social progress and better standards of life in larger freedom,

Whereas Member States have pledged themselves to achieve, in cooperation with the United Nations, the promotion of universal respect for and observance of human rights and fundamental freedoms,

Whereas a common understanding of these rights and freedoms is of the greatest importance for the full realization of this pledge,

Now, therefore,

The General Assembly

proclaims

This Universal Declaration of Human Rights

as a common standard of achievement for all peoples and all nations, to the end that every individual and every organ of society, keeping this Declaration constantly in mind, shall strive by teaching and education to promote respect for these rights and freedoms and by progressive measures, national and international, to secure their universal and effective recognition and observance, both among the peoples of Member States themselves and among the peoples of territories under their jurisdiction.

Article I

All human beings are born free and equal in dignity and rights. They are endowed with reason and conscience and should act towards one another in a spirit of brotherhood.

Article 2

Everyone is entitled to all the rights and freedoms set forth in this Declaration, without distinction of any kind, such as race, colour, sex, language, religion, political or other opinion, national or social origin, property, birth or other status.

Furthermore, no distinction shall be made on the basis of the political, jurisdictional or international status of the country or territory to which a person belongs, whether it be independent, trust, non-self-governing or under any other limitation of sovereignty.

Article 3

Everyone has the right to life, liberty and security of person.

Article 4

No one shall be held in slavery or servitude; slavery and the slave trade shall be prohibited in all their forms.

Article 5

No one shall be subjected to torture or to cruel, inhuman or degrading treatment or punishment.

Article 6

Everyone has the right to recognition everywhere as a person before the law.

Article 7

All are equal before the law and are entitled without any discrimination to equal protection of the law. All are entitled to equal protection against any discrimination in violation of this Declaration and against any incitement to such discrimination.

Article 8

Everyone has the right to an effective remedy by the competent national tribunals for acts violating the fundamental rights granted him by the constitution or by law.

Article 9

No one shall be subjected to arbitrary arrest, detention or exile.

Article 10

Everyone is entitled in full equality to a fair and public hearing by an independent and impartial tribunal, in the determination of his rights and obligations and of any criminal charge against him.

Article 11

(1) Everyone charged with a penal offence has the right to be presumed innocent until proved guilty according to law in a public trial at which he has had all the guarantees necessary for his defense.

(2) No one shall be held guilty of any penal offence on account of any act or omission, which did not constitute a penal offence, under national or international law, at the time when it was committed. Nor shall a heavier penalty be imposed than the one that was applicable at the time the penal offence was committed.

Article 12

No one shall be subjected to arbitrary interference with his privacy, family, home or correspondence, or to attacks upon his honor and reputation. Everyone has the right to the protection of the law against such interference or attacks.

Article 13

(1) Everyone has the right to freedom of movement and residence within the borders of each State.

(2) Everyone has the right to leave any country, including his own, and to return to his country.

Article 14

(1) Everyone has the right to seek and to enjoy in other countries asylum from persecution.

(2) This right may not be invoked in the case of prosecutions genuinely arising from non-political crimes or from acts contrary to the purposes and principles of the United Nations.

Article 15

(1) Everyone has the right to a nationality.

(2) No one shall be arbitrarily deprived of his nationality nor denied the right to change his nationality.

Article 16

(1) Men and women of full age, without any limitation due to race, nationality or religion, have the right to marry and to found a family. They are entitled to equal rights as to marriage, during marriage and at its dissolution.

(2) Marriage shall be entered into only with the free and full consent of the intending spouses.

(3) The family is the natural and fundamental group unit of society and is entitled to protection by society and the State.

Article 17

(1) Everyone has the right to own property alone as well as in association with others.

(2) No one shall be arbitrarily deprived of his property.

Article 18

Everyone has the right to freedom of thought, conscience and religion; this right includes freedom to change his religion or belief, and freedom, either alone or in community with others and in public or private, to manifest his religion or belief in teaching, practice, worship and observance.

Article 19

Everyone has the right to freedom of opinion and expression; this right includes freedom to hold opinions without interference and to seek, receive and impart information and ideas through any media and regardless of frontiers.

Article 20

(1) Everyone has the right to freedom of peaceful assembly and association.

(2) No one may be compelled to belong to an association.

Article 21

(1) Everyone has the right to take part in the government of his country, directly or through freely chosen representatives.

(2) Everyone has the right to equal access to public service in his country.

(3) The will of the people shall be the basis of the authority of government; this will shall be expressed in periodic and genuine elections,

which shall be by universal and equal suffrage and shall be held by secret vote or by equivalent free voting procedures.

Article 22

Everyone, as a member of society, has the right to social security and is entitled to realization, through national effort and international co-operation and in accordance with the organization and resources of each State, of the economic, social and cultural rights indispensable for his dignity and the free development of his personality.

Article 23

(1) Everyone has the right to work, to free choice of employment, to just and favorable conditions of work and to protection against unemployment.

(2) Everyone, without any discrimination, has the right to equal pay for equal work.

(3) Everyone who works has the right to just and favorable remuneration ensuring for himself and his family an existence worthy of human dignity,

and supplemented, if necessary, by other means of social protection.

(4) Everyone has the right to form and to join trade unions for the protection of his interests.

Article 24

Everyone has the right to rest and leisure, including reasonable limitation of working hours and periodic holidays with pay.

Article 25

(1) Everyone has the right to a standard of living adequate for the health and well-being of himself and of his family, including food, clothing, housing and medical care and necessary social services, and the right to security in the event of unemployment, sickness, disability, widowhood, old age or other lack of livelihood in circumstances beyond his control.

(2) Motherhood and childhood are entitled to special care and assistance. All children, whether born in or out of wedlock, shall enjoy the same social protection.

Article 26

(1) Everyone has the right to education. Education shall be free, at least in the elementary and fundamental stages. Elementary education shall be compulsory. Technical and professional education shall be made generally available and higher education shall be equally accessible to all on the basis of merit.

(2) Education shall be directed to the full development of the human personality and to the strengthening of respect for human rights and fundamental freedoms. It shall promote understanding, tolerance and friendship among all nations, racial or religious groups, and shall further the activities of the United Nations for the maintenance of peace.

(3) Parents have a prior right to choose the kind of education that shall be given to their children.

Article 27

(1) Everyone has the right freely to participate in the cultural life of the community, to enjoy the arts and to share in scientific advancement and its benefits.

(2) Everyone has the right to the protection of the moral and material interests resulting from any scientific, literary or artistic production of which he is the author.

Article 28

Everyone is entitled to a social and international order in which the rights and freedoms set forth in this Declaration can be fully realized.

Article 29

(1) Everyone has duties to the community in which alone the free and full development of his personality is possible.

(2) In the exercise of his rights and freedoms, everyone shall be subject only to such limitations as are determined by law solely for the purpose of securing due recognition and respect for the rights and freedoms of others and of meeting the just requirements of morality, public order and the general welfare in a democratic society.

(3) These rights and freedoms may in no case be exercised contrary to the purposes and principles of the United Nations.

Article 30

Nothing in this Declaration may be interpreted as implying for any State, group or person any right to engage in any activity or to perform any act aimed at the destruction of any of the rights and freedoms set forth herein."

Start of commentary (for those who fast forwarded):

Look at "Article 7" of the "Universal Declaration of Human Rights." It is "discrimination," according to the United Nations, when people from DSS and Doctors break a person's Constitutional Rights. Also, the 8th Article of the "Universal Declaration of Human Rights" says that: "Everyone has the right to an *effective remedy by the competent national tribunals* for acts violating the fundamental rights granted him by the Constitution or by law."

What ever happened to Dr. Martin Luther King's Dream where everyone is treated equal under the eyes of God— "EVERYONE!"? When people are silent about injustice, it just keeps getting worse and leads to tyranny.

To the US government:

STOP giving unequal treatment to moms and dads and families who need drug treatment, instead of destroying their families and state of livlihood. STOP violating the American Citizen's 4th and 8th Constitutional Amendment Rights:

The **Fourth Amendment** (**Amendment** IV) to the United States Constitution is the part of the Bill of Rights which guards against "unreasonable searches and seizures."

The **Eighth Amendment (Amendment** VIII) to the United States Constitution is the part of the Bill of Rights which guards against "excessive fines imposed, nor cruel and unusual punishments inflicted."

What is the solution? Base your actions in a non-biased manner. **Cut out the vindictiveness against people who do drugs (treat them like you would your family).** What would have happened if I were a Kennedy? It would be like it never happened. Is that fair?

You (the legal system) cause society more harm than good. You only need to break apart families in TRUE emergencies. Do it in a way that is confidential so people's careers aren't ruined; you push people into poverty by your public humiliation.

Moreover, if parents are doing drugs, they need to be put into a family support center where the whole family heals TOGETHER.

I am not going to go through the "Universal Declaration of Human Rights" line-by-line because I would be able to fill volumes. Make your own judgements. Hopefully you did read it and are able to think about events in your own life that just didn't seem right. You be the judge.

Chapter 11

Decriminalization of All Drugs:

ALL drugs need to be legal in this country on safe-haven reservations, similar to the Netherlands; simple possession also needs to be decriminalized to an extent. Why fight a battle you can NEVER win? What are the benefits? Wouldn't this cause more crime? Wouldn't it make life worse? No. Absolutely not! It would solve the majority of our problems actually.

I am not advocating recreational drug use in the least bit, I am offering a remedy; I am offering a legal way for those that need help to be able to seek it. I am offering a humanitarian way of dealing with people who do drugs, rather then dehumanizing them so they aren't accepted in our society. As it is today, a lot of people don't see people who do drugs as people. This is kind of like a soldier overseas that doesn't see the enemy as human beings. He just plucks them off one-by-one like he is having target practice. At least that is how they are trained, so there is no remorse.

The drug war needs to stop. Entire families are being murdered and/or tortured because they know something and a dealer is afraid they will snitch. Innocent bystanders are being caught in the cross-fire of a bullet intended to hit an addict who didn't pay up? We can protect society from drugs by isolating them to certain geographic boundries. The FDA can also regulate these illicit drugs to help addicts avoid drug death attributed to a bad batch.

Furthermore, we are empowering druglords and drug dealers; we are creating a great business nitch for them. Meanwhile, they are rising up and we are working as hard as we can and some of us can't get ahead. We need to legalize all drugs on reservations where all the profits go to the government.

The druglords would then have to work like regular people—same with the dealers. Then all the power would go to the United States and its citizens. We are empowering gangs, dealers and drug lords because of our war on drugs. We make the enemy stronger and ourselves weaker—every second of every day.

The United States of America will NEVER-EVER win the war on drugs. Furthermore, the United States of America is set on a path of self-destruction like the ancient Mayan civilization because of it's elite beliefs and "We know what's best for everybody" policy that are pushed on the rest of the world.

I have seen the dark side of America; the dark side is the countless damage caused by some of America's vindictive laws and actions by the elite people in power. I say, "Power to the people. Never-ever forget, the government works for us and we have the right to revolt when they are causing more harm to the populace than good."

To the US government and its citizens:

Accept people for who they are and give them the chance to handle their addictions legally. Addiction is very REAL. It is a disease. Also, being a drug addict or doing drugs on a recreational level does NOT mean you are a "child abuser."

Since drug addiction is a disease, if it ever gets beyond recreational use, legalizing drugs will help the diseased person in many ways. For one, it will provide financially reasonable costs for the drug. If the "user" cannot afford the drug anymore, we can offer community service work to pay for their addiction. Isn't that better then having them desparately looking for money and robbing possibly your son or daughter (or you)? Isn't that better than paying for their room and board in jail?

Also, remember that street drugs have impurities sometimes that cause death or severe sickness. Since addiction is a disease, do you think that it is fair for a human being to have to resort to taking big risks and possibly losing their life? What if this disease hit your son or daughter? In addition, do you think it is fair to have your child, possibly, performing sexual favors to get another fix? Would you want them to come up HIV positive? Moreover, these drug addicts then go out and spread Aids, Herpes and other STD's to unsuspecting partners.

Would you like your son or daughter to get Aids from a drug addict? You will respond, "My son or daughter wouldn't be hanging around those type of people." My counter response comes in the form of a couple hypothetical scenarios: What if one of those drug addicts got back on their feet somehow and cleaned up their act? Then your son or daughter works with them serving tables while getting through college. That drug addict isn't going to tell of their sordid past. One night your son or daughter might hook up with this person who has Aids. The condom breaks. Guess what? Welcome to the Aids epidemic.

You may say that this scenario won't happen to your son or daughter. Be careful with what you think may or may not happen because the future is uncertain and anything is possible. Here is another quick scenario: The addict who contracted Aids performs a sexual act on a dealer to get another hit (of crack or whatever). That dealer then finds a longterm female companion and gives them Aids, after he contracted it from the addict doing him a sexual favor. Then, the dealer and his woman have a baby that is HIV positive at birth. How often does our government give children HIV indirectly by not helping drug addicts?

These scenarios may sound out there to you, but the point is truly that we are contributing to the spread of Aids. You may not see it, but it is real. Many people are being infected that otherwise wouldn't if my vision came to fruition.

My solution would help the spread of Aids— simply putting drug addicts to work doing jobs that nobody wants. Who cares if they are using the money for drugs? The drug addict is then helping out the community instead of bothering you on the street for money. Again, drug addiction is a disease and we are talking about real human beings.

Furthermore, people who use drugs are taking big risks if they don't have a trusted dealer. I have personally been mugged 7 times. I will tell you about one in particular: I had already been robbed twice that night when I pulled into the hood looking for crack cocaine. I came upon a group of gang-looking African-Americans. I pulled the car over and rolled down my window. One of them jumped on the trunk of my car, just messing with me. I showed no fear.

I asked if they knew where I could get some rock. One of them said, "I have it right here in my hand. Give me the money and I'll give you the rock." I kept wanting to see it, but he wouldn't let me. I then got out of the car and said, "Give me the rock and I'll give you the money." He said, "I think you are the police! Give me the money first."

I then said, "I'm going," and proceeded to get back in my car. He somehow finally convinced me to give him the money as he gave me the rock at the same time. When I did this, two of the African-Americans reached in the front passenger window stripping me of all my possessions. They then ran off and were almost instantly out of sight. The point is that buying drugs on the streets is dangerous; I could've been killed—like some people are. In addition, I know of people who were in a similar predicament and actually killed their robbers. That was wrong of them in the sense that the punishment didn't fit the crime, but those people (the robbers)--who have devastated families now--would otherwise still be alive.

I also wanted to add a unique perspective in that I taught at the elementary school that had the highest poverty-rate in the district. I can't even begin to tell you how many students each year lost a dad, uncle, brother or other loved one due to drug-related murder. I had one student who lost two uncles in the same week in separate incidents. When the police came to my school to do an assembly, they asked how many students had witnessed a murder. About 60-70 percent of the hands were raised.

Many of the students would begin to tell me how their dad or uncle was murdered. Some were dragged to death tied to a rope at the back of a car. Some were shot, and others were stabbed. I would have to stop the kids before I knew too much and then I could have been in danger; a lot of these kids are witness to many things they should not see just by virtue of living in a particular neighborhood. Most of these kids know they or their family will be in serious trouble if they snitch, but kids are kids and something might slip out.

I can truly tell you, after personally knowing many drug dealers with children: most drug dealers would like a normal job, college and an honest life for their kids. Again, once a felon, always a felon. There is very little forgiveness in this country when it comes to finding work.

Getting back to all the unnecessary drug-related murders that happen daily in this country. What motivates the murderers to kill their victims? Here are some of the reasons:

1. Snitching

2. Knowing too much

3. Being witness to a crime

4. Unpaid debts

5. Jealousy between dealers

6. Competition of territory

   between dealers

7. Proving loyalty

8. Getting robbed

Again, if drugs were legal in certain safe-zones, we wouldn't be seeing all this murder that I believe to be mostly drug-related. What if a stray bullet shot your child, mother or grandmother? That would almost never happen if drugs were federally controlled in certain geographic zones. If we don't enact my solution, are you really ok with this type of random murder in our country when we have the power to prevent it?

Getting back to being brainwashed by the media, it is ok to have reservations about my ideas. That is how you have been programmed. My ideas may sound scary, but I'm telling you, the government is probably controlling the feelings you have about my vision. Have the courage to break that control. You need to be in control of how you truly feel and what you think is best for the good of humanity.

If you read this and feel sorry for me or think all my ideas to be ridiculous, read on. You will see that my ideas are right. Toward the end of this book, I found a country that has decriminalized all drugs since 2001. Everything I said about the spread of Aids to drug users dying of bad batches…it was all true, as crazy as it may sound.

Chapter 12

Suicide Note:

The day my children got taken, along with my career that I spent 8 years working on, my psychological well-being became severely troubled. Take note, because I am just one victim of many. My expressions can be the beginning of the research that proves what taking children from their parents can do to their psychology.

I tried to kill myself by overdosing on drugs many times since this major crime against humanity occurred. One time, I took an entire bottle of Xanax with about $1,000 in crack. It obviously didn't work; maybe God needs me to start a movement.

Here is a suicide note I wrote after taking a bottle of prescription sleeping pills and after a big crack binge. In addition, I faded out on my bed to a cord wrapped multiple times around my neck. The light was off; I had a lighter in my left hand and a pencil in my right. The actual note has sloppy writing for this reason, not to mention I didn't have a hard surface to write on (I will fill in the blanks in the Director's Cut—that is if I ever get to a point when I feel that its release will ONLY serve to better humanity and help psychologists in their research):

"I want the world to know that the ONLY reason why I… _____, _____, and Dr. _____ …is because the media manipulators would just make me out to be a crazy drug addict. In reality, [some social workers and some delivery doctors] these people are evil monsters that destroy children and ruin people's lives. They truly…... I know too much and can't live with children being abused and sometimes murdered in foster care as the real parents are vindictively destroyed. Why are we letting this happen in our country? People believe the lies. Good-bye everybody. Hopefully my death will help prevent further acts of inhumanity.

Suicide Note
_-_-10
2:11AM"

It is important to note that I have deeply reflected on the belief that my perpetrators deserved physical harm. Again, let me remind you that every man has his breaking point. At that breaking point, man is capable of murder. You can't judge me because you have never walked in my shoes. Furthermore, I never carried out any heinous acts of revenge.

These violators need simple justice in the order of fines against their livelihood to go toward the victims. I know they were just doing there jobs, in a vindictive manner, but so were the Nazis who were punished at the Nuremberg trials.

These Nazis were eventually sentenced to death. Instead of using a long rope, they were then hanged by a short rope (it is believed to have made them suffer more, but the US denies those allegations as they always deny anything that makes them look bad).

Incidentally, one of the indictments included "Crimes against humanity." That is my specific allegation against certain parts of the United States legal system. Remember that I love my country, but I also believe that certain people need to be brought to justice. However, I would NOT hang them. I would, again, do the right thing by fining them and/or sentencing them to a small amount of jail time.

Hitler was wrong and we shouldn't make his same mistakes. I can only speculate, but he probably felt deeply wronged by the Jews and snapped. He should NEVER have had the Holocaust. That was SO wrong of him; remember that I am a humanitarian seeking to do the right thing.

There is one more thing I have to say in this chapter because it is the most appropriate place to put it. People might wonder why I didn't just blow my brains out with a gun? Why didn't I just sit in my garage with the car running? Why didn't I jump off a bridge or commit suicide by cop? These are all real good questions.

I thought about every possible method of suicide and what it all boiled down to was my preferred method was death by overdose. It's that simple. So if a guy is doing massive amounts of drugs and going for death, you can probably understand why he did so much.

Chapter 13

My Apparent Death (The 4th Amendment was Actually Followed for Once):

Let me take you back to a time when I had been up almost 2 weeks straight on a suicidal crack binge. By the way, I was never like this before—I believe that my behavior can be explained by complete rage, Post Traumatic Stress Disorder, temporary insanity, the loss of the will to live and clouded judgment. Anyway, I was driving my car to meet my dealer for another $400. I came to a stop sign just by where I was meeting him.

Since I had been up for such a long period of time, I needed to rest. I pulled my car to where I was supposed to meet him. The next thing I know, I opened my eyes to a paramedic pounding on my window. I looked around to see a big crowd of people, a couple cop cars, an ambulance and several officials of some kind.

I opened my door to the paramedic asking me if I knew what was going on. I truly thought I was still at that stop sign driving my car and I came upon an accident. He said, "No. This is all for you. A neighbor saw you 'still' in your car and thought you were dead." He then asked me what year it was and so on. After he was convinced that I was ok, he said, "Let me ask you this? Some cops would like to know what all that money is for on your passengers seat?"

At this point I thought quickly and told him that I was on prescription Xanax, which was true. I told him that I felt too sleepy to be behind the wheel and pulled over for a nap. I then told him that it was kind of embarrassing, but I was intending to use the money at a porn store right around the corner.

He said that my story made perfect sense, since the porn store truly was a block away. He then had me sign some papers that officially released me from his care. Little did they know that I had a crack pipe between my legs that had crack resign in it. Thanks to these officials following the 4th Amendment, I was sent on my way. If they violated it however, I would have gone to jail for a long time.

Would that have helped anyone? Remember the butterfly effect? There are people in jail right now who are there for simple possession, who had to defend themselves from being raped. They then killed their rapist--in the heat of defending themselves--and are now in jail for the rest of their lives or awaiting Capital punishment. Don't ever forget about these very real victims who have families that care about them; some children will never know their father because of these types of injustices.

Chapter 14

Letters:

Some of these letters have dates and some do not. I tried to arrange them in a somewhat organized fashion. It is especially important to note the letters to and from the ACLU (American Civil Liberties Union). I want to give the ACLU huge thanks for their role to help end segregation, as well as everything else they have done for the citizens of this country who were facing an injustice. You are America's angel when the Bill of Rights needs an amendment or is being abused and/or the laws need to be changed:

Your website received a form submission. Below are the results.

Comments about your request: I thought it was a violation of a pregnant women's 4th amendment right to be drug tested in the hospital without consent and then share that with the police. My children got taken away today. Let me know if you want the opportunity for a good case.

You may call my office on Monday and schedule an appointment.

Dear _____,

Thank you for contacting me with regard to your potential claim involving your wife's physician and decision to drug test. At this time, however, I must decline representation with regard to this action, as it is matter that is outside my areas of practice.

It was a pleasure speaking with you and I am sorry I was unable to assist you with this particular matter. I will be performing no legal services on your behalf.

Please bookmark www.CharlestonSCLawyer.com if the need for

an attorney should arise in the future. I welcome the opportunity to be of service to you, your friends or family and if I can't assist with your legal problem, I will certainly refer you to someone I know and trust.

Regards,

_____

Subject: Violation of the 4th Amendment Rights
Body:
There was no reason whatsoever that the hospital should have tested my wife
for drugs when she went in for labor. They did not tell her until social
services showed up and said he was taking our children unless I tested
negative. I tested positive for cocaine, which was a bad decision on my part
and I wont do it again. The police just took my children now. I live in a
small town and I will now be ruined. My life is going to be destroyed. My
wife and I won't do drugs again. I am infuriated over her rights being
violated though. Please let me know how you feel about this.

6-5-10

Dear mom,

Something that I should tell you that you probably already know is that I actually believe different than many people in our nation. I certainly would run the country down a very successful road if I could help the President and Congress.

I'm actually thinking about Blitzkrieging my movement into action all across the nation, but only after I don't have to depend on an employer for my financial needs--I don't want to lose my job (since I may be misunderstood in regard to my views on some controversial subjects). The cool thing is that when I get independently wealthy I can speak my mind in any public forum because we are protected by the 1st Amendment (Freedom of Speech). I am in the process of writing a book based on my philosophy and beliefs, not that far off from the Netherlands system of government.

I am hoping one day to truly advise the President (even though the Presidency isn't enough in itself for positive change to occur) and change our nation similar to the Netherlands way of handling the war on drugs--it is the right thing to do even though you probably can't see what I see yet.

I believe that we are on a self-destructive path and one day we will be taken out by Russia, China, Iran, North Korea and/or other countries that are sick and tired of our invasive and controlling ways. I love my country so much--that is why I want to save it from getting annihilated in WW III.

I believe my philosophy and beliefs are very futuristic and will take place in 50-500 years any way. I feel like I am stuck in the past, like I'm from the future, because I clearly see things so different than most people. I know I'm not crazy, I believe that I am extremely intelligent and have an infinitely deep humanitarian-heart.

I can't share my book with you yet because I don't want my ideas stolen over the Internet. It is brilliant though and I am very excited about it! Once I am done pouring all my ideas, beliefs and philosophy of my Saving America Act, I will let you read and edit it.

6-9-10

Dear ACLU,

I am writing you with the hopes of making an ally toward my future political motives. I can't do much right now because I'm not independently wealthy yet--I don't want to lose my job. However, during this time I am in the process of writing a book that outlines my beliefs, ideas, vision and philosophy.

I believe that we are on a self-destructive path as a nation, similar to the ancient Mayans, and we won't survive going in the same direction. I already see many nations preparing for taking us out in WW III. I know you think that is extreme, but we have always been a nation of "We know what's best for everybody in the world."

We are and always have been too invasive in the livelihood of peoples and nations. Consequently, peoples' liberty and right to person is taken away and many innocent people's lives are destroyed when there is so many other peaceful ways of solving our problems.

Did you know that according to the United Nations, I have the right to hold "competent national tribunals against" certain persons that violated my 4th and 8th Amendment Rights, not to mention the many violations of the "Articles of Universal Declaration of Human Rights?"

I plan on eventually advising the highest office of power our government has to offer. I was once VP and President of a student body of 15,000 at my college in which I was successfully voted in both times--I have the background and experience that it is going to take.

My experience with DSS has opened my eyes to so many things we are doing inhumanely to our people and the people of the world. We need to be a nation of peace and treat each other as family, yet still offer the capitalistic dream. Our soldiers aren't spilling their blood for a facade of falsehood. We owe them more than that.

I am ready now to advise the President and achieve national and world peace, but I want to wait till my book is published on the New York Times #1 Seller's List first. Then, I will be ready.

At that time, I will need the ACLU to work with me toward achieving my goals, which I won't share with you yet--I just ask that you have an open mind when you read it. I hope I sparked your interest for when it is a worldwide success. Sincerely,

_____

6-15-10

To DSS (_____, _____ and _____) and Dr._____:

I forgive all the harm you brought to my family and for all your crimes against humanity. At this point, it's between you and God and possibly the "competent national tribunals for acts violating the fundamental rights granted him by the constitution or by law." (The United Nations) I only ask you this: When you meet your maker and He asks, "Why?" What will you say to Him?

Dear _____,

I was one of the attorneys that handled the Ferguson case, so I do know these issues. I was serious when I said that we could be helpful to your attorney in the DSS case. Getting your kids home ASAP has to be the priority.

Staff Attorney
ACLU SC National Office

From: _____
Sent: Wednesday, February 17, 2010 11:49 PM
To:
Subject: One More Thing

Dear ACLU,

Again, thanks for your response. I really appreciate you taking so much time and interest in my situation. As I stated in my letter, "I will dedicate my life to this cause." If you ever decide that you want to set that precedent and think you can actually pull it off, I would love to be a major supporter.

Right now, my kids are what matters most, but I personally believe that our society is becoming too Big Brother and that destroys lives. The legal system causes more harm than good in many situations. I personally feel that justice needs to be served with this Doctor for playing God with my life and deciding what is best for my children, but legally I can't (at least at this juncture in history).

Again, thank you so much and I appreciate your willingness to look into my complaint, as well as, the genuine response I needed from the expert I was looking near and far to find.

Sincerely,

_____

From: Staff Attorney (ACLU)

To: _____

Sent: Wed, February 17, 2010 11:22:26 AM

Subject: See attached response

Staff Attorney

ACLU SC National Office

South Carolina National Office

P.O. Box 20998

Charleston, SC 29413-0998

www.aclusouthcarolina.org

February 17, 2010

By email to _____

Dear _____:

Thank you for contacting the ACLU South Carolina. I know that you want your children home as soon as possible.

The ACLU is a private, non-profit organization that seeks to protect the rights guaranteed in the U.S. Constitution, particularly those listed in the Bill of Rights. We look for cases involving civil liberties that will affect a large number of people, set a new precedent, or decide an issue of law. We rarely undertake the representation of individuals in a tort cases involving the determination of contested facts.

Your first priority needs to be the return of your children. You may already have an attorney in your DSS case. If you do not, you need to obtain representation in that case as soon as possible. ACLU-SC cannot represent you in the DSS case. We have resources that might be helpful to whoever does represent you. Feel free to have your attorney in the DSS case contact me.

While you may have a complaint against the physician, it is not quite the same as the *Ferguson* case as it does not appear that the search was used for criminal purposes. The odds are that a consent for treatment was signed which allowed the doctor to order any tests he thought necessary. The issue is probably not whether he had authority to order the test, but whether he had a duty to report the results, which was sufficient to allow him to reveal information to the DSS that would otherwise have been private information. That is not an easy question to answer.

It is also possible that DSS had no right to demand that you submit to a drug test. That is, of course, a separate matter.

Underlying all these issues is DSS's position that a single drug test without any additional investigation is proof that a parent is unfit. That is a larger policy issue. Lives of children around the state are being turned upside down by that policy. The ACLU-SC is researching that issue and may devise a legal strategy to attack it in the future. If you would like to be informed of our future actions in relationship to

DSS, let me know and I will put you on our contact list.

I would also suggest that you request copies of your wife's hospital file and your DSS file as soon as possible. Anyone who undertakes your representation will benefit from having those documents to review.

The bottom line is that you need a legal strategy to get your family back together. Once your children are returned to you, then, you will have plenty of time to determine what additional legal action you may take.

Sincerely,

. . . .

Staff attorney

ACLU

Feb. 17

To Whom It May Concern,

I am _____'s mother. I will be arriving in South Carolina on March 8th or sooner if you need me for testing. His wife's mother will be leaving on the 9th and I will be taking over as a supervisor of the children. I will stay as long as it takes.

I do have a request; my mother who just got out of the hospital in Florida is 86 years old and the Great Grandmother of the two kids. She is weak and I need to go see her. I would love to take the kids to Florida on March 25th and return on the 31st of March. If I cannot do this I understand. If I can't I will fly my husband in from California to be the supervisor of the children until I return from Florida.

I am willing to stay in South Carolina as long as it takes. My son said it possibly would be 3 to 6 months. I will do what needs to be done.

My husband and I do not do drugs, we don't drink or smoke and we are willing to take any test required either here in California or when we arrive in South Carolina.

We love our son, daughter-in-law and grandchildren. Please let us help them.

Thanks,

.....

Dear ACLU,

Thanks again for your interest and help. To give you an update, I have lost my career as a teacher; my wife and I are staying in an apartment for 6 months while my mom is out here from California to act as guardian at our house; there is now a risk of us losing our home because now I am working as a server and paying for apartment rent and a mortgage. Also, my 7-year-old daughter who used to practically be a straight A role model student is now expressing that she will kill herself (actually held scissors to her throat--saying that she feels mistreated by DSS). We are in the process of getting my daughter counseling (she has major anger issues).

I left a message for our court appointed attorney to call you. His name is _____.

Thank you so much,

_____

Dear ACLU,

Since I have last corresponded, my wife got full custody and is taking the children out of state. I have gotten my teaching credential suspended for 3 years. I have met many parents in my classes from _____ Hospital that got tested unconstitutionally. One parent had her children beaten, causing scars forever, while in foster care. One parent used to work for the same Doctor that violated my wife's 4th Amendment right and got her baby taken. Then she was thrown against the wall, fired and arrested in the hospital--after the Dr. breached a contract that said nothing would happen if she fessed up. In addition, a couple in my parenting class got their baby taken away for the mom being overheard saying, "I can't afford formula." That baby died last night while in foster care. I was thinking we could do a class action lawsuit against the hospital for breaking the 4th Amendment, and working hand-in-hand with DSS and the police to get their babies taken away.

I have wondered why so many children are being taken in this area. Almost all the parents have to do a psychological evaluation and the Doctor's doing that might be profiting--it cost $400 each. Also, the drug help places and parenting classes would go out of business if there weren't enough clients--just taking a wild guess. Also, DSS probably needs a certain number of cases a month to keep up with their budget and prevent layoffs. Please let me know if you would like to pursue this matter. I have all kinds of people who are victims that would absolutely hop aboard.

Sincerely,

_____

Dear ACLU,

I understand why you guys probably don't want to take my case anymore, because I didn't follow through like a caring parent should (I believe I went insane). That's ok. I was out of my head and very rebellious knowing that the majority of child abuse occurs in foster homes and really went off the deep end, also knowing my wife was the safety net and my kids would be ok in her hands.

All I have to do is complete a drug plan and I will be given rights to be alone with my kids again and my wife will come home from California [since this was written, she is gone for good and has full power of giving me my rights back—if approved by a family court judge]. I just wanted to say society probably won't accept my case, even at the Supreme Court level, because it seems that I have proven to be everything DSS has labeled me.   People just judge though and they would really have no idea unless it happened to them.

I was ready to end my life in the form of dying for this cause, as warped and disconnected as that may seem--based on my actions. I now have come to a point that it is no longer healthy for me to live in a world of rage against who I believe are abusing children far above and beyond parents doing drugs.

I just wanted to say that I am ready to move on. However, the battle now lies solely with you. I may not be the martyr I truly had set out to be--somehow hoping my death of a drug overdose or going to jail for absolute rebellion against the system would make me. I just want to say that you are the only hope to save these children and the only way is to change the law so that parents aren't continually being violated against their 4th Amendment right, knowing the children may end up dead in foster care, or badly abused--in some cases with permanent gashes across their face.

I just hope that you find it within yourself to see that society assumes that when you get your kids taken away you are a monster, when in fact most of these parents are really good people who would have benefited more from somebody helping and guiding them rather then the absolute destruction of their lives--and throwing their children into the lion's den. I know that is a hard battle to fight, knowing that society doesn't see the true reality of that dark and horrific world. I also know that these laws got voted in because society honestly was trying to do what was best.

If I were in your position, I would gather real statistics of the amount of abuses in foster care and accidental deaths of foster kids, mostly blamed on SIDS, and prove that the majority of these happen in foster homes as opposed to the few and far between cases that happen in the homes of the biological parents.

Like I said, I am stepping out. I need to get my life back on track and I can no longer live with such extreme rage or I cannot be happy and it will undoubtedly lead me down a very destructive path. You don't have to write me back, I just wish you the best of luck and truly hope that you can make a positive change to help the innocent children from being psychologically damaged for life.

In fact, a lot of parents in the system were foster kids themselves and the long-term damage in my opinion will be an endless cycle. When foster kids feel abandoned by their parents and abused by the system, I have seen time and time again that they grow up to have their kids taken by the system.

Once more, after you have your kids taken by DSS, you are a monster to society. This pushes people even further into poverty and makes a much worse situation of society wanting to have its vengeance and continually setting out against you, even when you do get your kids back. Please help protect the children and families from the current laws so that this horrific reality will go away.

In the name of humanity,

_____

Here is a quoted letter I just found in my vacant oldest daughter's room (It was probably written when relatives were in and out of my home serving as the foster parents of my children, as I was living in an apartment with my wife):

"Please lisin to me do you Know Why I been crying because I cant stop thiking abot me getting taken away and getting the srack a yo get spling"—not sure what this means, but when I asked my daughter over the phone she said that it probably means when she was in foster care her head kept spinning. Something else I should add is that she told me it could have something to do with "it was snowing."

We hadn't had snow in South Carolina in years and the night my children were kidnapped, it got very dark and cold and it snowed. I remember standing out in my backyard lit by floodlights, looking up at the night-sky with both my arms outstretched. The snowflakes were melting on my faced-up palms and face. I remember thinking it was my children's first snow in South Carolina and how metaphorically ice-cold it must have been for them to be held up in a secret location, in the hands of strangers--with no right to contact their parents.

"But mostly what Im crying about is if we dint move from Calfonya these woud of never hapend to us or yo giys. Please lisin to what im saying."

I love you mom, Dad

If you bring up a letter like this to the Department of Social Services, the most common response that I've heard goes something like this:

"Most children don't know they are victims of their parents. We are serving in their best interest even if they don't accept it. This phenomenon can simply be explained by the 'Stockholm Syndrome' where victims who are kidnapped express adulation toward their kidnapper."

Getting down to the psychological aspects of this innocent child psychologically raped by the system, you could see that she clearly has nothing but love for her parents. The system took it upon themselves to dub her parents "child abusers" simply because of the positive results of drugscreens that were technically conducted unconstitutionally, if you believe in the 4th Amendment.

If you look deeper into the psychological aspects of my daughter during the time of this letter, you will see a child desparately crying out for help. Remember, this innocent child that was dehumanized by our government, would later threaten and intend to carry out murder against her perpetrators (in reference to when she wanted to kill her Guardian ad Litem with a knife); she would almost take her own life with pointed scissors; and much later down the road she would threaten to murder a child at school and then proceed to get into a physical fight with her. In one class the teacher had to isolate her because she couldn't get along with the other children.

How can anyone say that all of this psychological damage is worth removing a child from their home due to parents testing positive for drugs? There is NO justification. Children who are truly being abused by their parents SHOULD BE removed from their homes if there is direct evidence of the alledged abuse.

Recreational drug use is hard to justify to the American public. However, what I can say is that it shoud be treated as a separate matter, rather than finding the parents automatically guilty of child abuse. If you read some of the letters from the ACLU, you will see that they actually agree with me. Read these letters carefully. Remember that the ACLU is the MOST powerful civil rights organization in the world.

Getting back to my daughter. I would first like to say that this book is written *live* and what I mean by that is at the time of me writing it, I touch upon sporadic events that are current in my life. Just now (less than 3 minutes ago), I received a call from my daughter, 3000 miles away—who I haven't seen in about 5 or 6 months (not sure—I've lost track of the time).

She called me from my inlaws' house completely devastated and almost hysterically crying to the point that I could barely understand her. She is broken. The system broke my daughter. If you support against child abuse, always remember that the system conducts the majority of the abuse. If you believe that and you support against child abuse, then you are empowering the Department of Social Services to continually destroy families and ruin children's lives.

Stop. Before you get infuriated at me, I am aware that there are real child abusers other than the US government. All I'm saying is that we need to change the Department of Social Services now. Also, it's the right thing to do to support against child abuse, but support it in a way that doesn't further empower the government to abuse children.

Getting back to my daughter. Let me reemphasize that she made almost all A's and I had her set up to get into the Magnet program. Think of what kind of amazing future she could have had if the system didn't rape her dignity and sense of security. I personally believe she is entitled to $10,000,000 or more from the government. Who knows? Maybe one day there will be a class action lawsuit holding the government responsible for victimizing children and families and EVERY victim will get a chunk. However, make no mistake, no amount of money nor any type of material possession could ever bring a rape victim back to normal health. I use the word "rape" in a psychological sense.

Yes I said it, and I mean it too. It is important to note that I am not being overdramatic; remember that I hold a Master's Degree in Education and I worked with thousands of children throughout my career. I consider myself somewhat of an expert when it comes to child psychology.

We are talking about real children and real psychological rapes that damage them for life. Remember the butterfly effect? The future is uncertain and as a result of being abused as children, there is no telling what actions they may take later down the road because of their troubled psyches.

Chapter 15

Hitler's America:

We turn on the TV and watch sports, sitcoms and other shows of entertainment. We then watch the news, which is really just a tool to shape and mold you into how the government wants you to be. We are all just zombies and the TV is our God.

Have you ever stopped to ponder what may be going on right under your nose, as you sip your beer during Monday Night Football? Probably not, because people don't usually think—they just want to be accepted by friends and society and they go with the flow. There is nothing wrong with football, the point is just that if you go to a friend's house to watch the game, you find yourself cheering and getting into it because you do what is natural to fit in.

So what happens when one of us follows our own system of beliefs, which may not be approved of by the norm? The legal system sets out to destroy you because if you don't follow their guidelines you are a threat to their control.   We are a nation of "We know what's best for other people." That simply means that if someone isn't like the majority, we will bully them until they are; in many cases some people refuse to conform because they don't think they are doing anything wrong and they aren't hurting anyone but themselves.

Look at my life for instance. My wife went into labor and was tested by the Dr. in a vindictive manner. I say "vindictive" because the Dr. and the hospital don't even bother to tell the woman she is being drug tested. The woman doesn't even have the right to sign a form giving her permission, which technically goes against the 4th Amendment right. An informative flyer would be nice.

She was positive for marijuana (even though the baby was negative); the Department of Social Services them comes in to take the kids, unless the father shows up negative. In my case I was positive too. The government then decided to dub me a "child abuser" in court, take my children and destroy my teaching career.

Have you ever thought what Hitler would do if you didn't completely conform to his Nazi ways? For instance, maybe you practiced Judaism. It didn't hurt anybody else, but you were still sought after and destroyed.

I once had the chance to visit Mauthasuen in Austria. It was one of the last concentration camps to be liberated by US soldiers during the time of WW II. I saw the "Stairs of Death," which were ridiculously steep steps that were almost too many to go up even in perfect health. The Jews had to carry boulders up them and would then fall to their deaths once they could no longer go on. If a Jew dropped his or her boulder, they were plucked off by Nazi artillery.

There was also a cliff atop a very shallow pond filled with rocks. The Jews would be lined up at the top of the cliff and have to push the person in front of them off to their crushing deaths. Most people probably don't want to hear the truth, but I am going to tell it like it is; this book is what is keeping me going and my mission is to share my point of view with the world.

What happened in my case is I was the Jew in WW II Nazi Germany, metaphorically speaking. I chose to do drugs, which didn't hurt anyone but myself. I was then given a boulder and told to climb the stairs of death. The government then came in and completely tore apart my life. They destroyed my perfect family and made sure I would lose my teaching job. This would then lead toward a possible foreclosure and bankruptcy. Ultimately, my own wife who had finally turned against me pushed me off the cliff.

Let me ask you this? Who did I ever hurt? Are you telling me that if someone buys drugs and does them in a hotel room away from anyone they could damage, it constitutes destroying them and their family? Absolutely! You may never do drugs and slough this off thinking it doesn't affect you, but how selfish must you be?

I can go on and on about other people who have been destroyed like me, but what did we ever do to deserve all that? I charge the legal system with criminal acts of inhumanity against its citizens. The legal system completely destroyed my life, so why am I not a terrorist? I believe I have too much to share to want to kill myself and other people. Besides, it is hard for me to kill people--even though they killed my family and me (metaphorically).

Have you ever stopped to think about why terrorists are so pissed off? Do you think they were born Satan spawn and are just inherently evil? The media and legal system will tell you they are "evil doers." In fact, I talked to a lady last night that said, "If we don't kill them, they will kill us." She even said they aren't even human. Really?

What the legal system won't tell you is the crimes of inhumanity our government possibly committed against them. If thousands of others like me are never heard and we are citizens of this country, do you really think our media and legal system will tell us the whole truth about American Hitlerism in other countries?

Let me ask you this? Are you truly proud to be a citizen of this country? Chances are that your answer is yes. I am too, for the most part—I only have a problem with the injustices committed by our legal system both domestically and abroad. Everything else is awesome! In fact, *I believe that if the government used my ideas it would lead to our country being the most powerful in the world, as well as the ability to sustain that power throughout the ages—not to mention we will finally be respected by most other countries.*

Desperate change is needed to stop the injustices that are currently going on in our country. I guarantee that if we continue to be as an invasive country to our own citizens and the citizens of other countries, we will fall like Rome—it is only a matter of time.

Chapter 16

A White Power Government to Oppress the Black Community:

Back in the eighties, the origin of the crack movement, there has been a well-known conspiracy theory that the CIA helped bring massive amounts of cocaine into the United States. Look at senator John Kerry's (if you don't know, he once ran for President of the United States) investigation that alleges top officials of our government not only supported this movement, but also turned a blind eye to help bring down black America. Why would our government do that? This is a theory that cannot be proved, but do your research; there are a lot of people out there that believe this and believe there was a major cover up.

Look what happened during Hurricane Katrina. Why was FEMA (Federal Emergency Management Agency) so unresponsive while dozens of black communities were suffering and dying daily? President Bush says it hurt his feelings when Kanye West said that he "hates black people." What if the majority of communities in Louisiana were white middle-class? Would the timeliness of response have been different?

Look back at the rap group NWA that sparked the rap movement. Black leaders of the Compton, California community (Dr. Dre., Ice Cube, Eazy-E...) finally started calling it like it is. During that time, there were massive accounts of racist white police in the Southern California area who were beating black people with billy clubs without justification and getting away with it. Then the Rodney King beating was caught on tape and sparked the L.A. riots. I overlooked the riots from a mountaintop where I lived at the time. I was there.

It is clearly obvious throughout American history that the white government believed itself to be superior (kind of like Hitler believed the Aryan race to be superior). We have tried and tried as a nation to oppress black people.

I can tell you from personal experience that if I didn't know anyone in an area who could sell me crack, I would drive the streets looking. I can personally attest to how it is in Los Angeles, California and in parts of South Carolina. Did you know that if I were up to bat, I NEXT-to-NEVER had three strikes? Within asking three black people if they sold crack, I would find at least one that could pull out a bag from his or her pocket and take my money. This isn't an open invite for the "Myth Busters;" lets just say I have experience on who looks like they can be carrying crack.

In light of the above statements I've made, I want to take my point of view even further. The kidnapping of children by the Department of Social Services is out of control and they typically prey upon children at the poverty level. I happened to be a fluke, as they admitted to me time and time again.

Since I had the opportunity to be on the inside and meet with dozens and dozens of parents in my parenting classes and DSS mandated drug-rehab classes, I have formed a possible theory--this particular theory is admittedly far-fetched, but it was true in my mind at the time and I want to keep it in my book to challenge people to think through all angles of reality. Maybe the white officials who helped put together DSS wanted to target African-American babies with intent to brainwash them and peel away their cultural heritage? What if the foster parents were black? It doesn't matter. It would still take away any pride and cultural aspects the parents would have wanted to hand down to their children. It would also place the children with conformists.

Look at our history, when we overpowered the Native Americans back at the start of our country, we started schools and hired teachers to strip them of their culture and force them to be like us. There is a term to describe this phenomenon called "deculturalization." During slavery we would strip black people of their cultural heritage, as the slaves would desperately try to hang on by making songs that would unite them as a group. These songs would have strong religious ties to their home of Africa. Overseers would ban any dancing, clapping of the hands, singing and so on, with intent to disunite the black community.

Now, let me take you forward a few centuries to the election of Barack Obama as the first black President of the United States. Is it possible that we came to a point in US history when we needed to appease the black community to reduce racial tension between them and the US government? I taught a majority of black children both before and after the election and can tell you it truly made them feel like they were finally a part of our country. We were at a point in American history where rap became the most influential music and the government was actually scared of the black community revolting? Rap music was and is very powerful and forever will be. It has the power to influence the way a lot of people feel and act, almost beyond the government's control.

I truly don't know the answer to the above question; however, like I said in my "Forward," I want to challenge you to think in ways outside what you are fed by the media. I want you to open your eyes to alternate realities that hold weight and truth. I want you to see beyond the facade of government propaganda. We need to finally follow our Constitution and the "Universal Declaration of Human Rights" and put an end to injustice in our country.

Chapter 17

Toe-to-Toe with My Children's Kidnapper?

_____, _____, _____…that name hits hard at my soul. I remember the broken promises after he stole my kids. He promised that the foster parents were "hand picked." That was a lie.

The first foster parent forgot my child at school and my daughter had to be removed to another foster parent that walked around naked (naked lady). She also gave my daughter cold baths and refused to leave the room, even though my daughter expressed that she was uncomfortable.

By the way, my daughter says that she was only allowed to fill the bath up less than halfway. On the other hand, she said her foster mom got full baths that were warm. I asked how she knew that and she said that she would be in the bathroom with her.

Promise number 2: "Trust me, your newborn and other daughter won't go into different homes." About two weeks later, with DSS refusing to answer any questions about our children's well being, we were told they were in separate homes. My oldest daughter was having enough trouble as it was accepting a baby sister and we thought this would bond them together. Wrong!

Promise number 3: "This kind of thing happens all the time. Don't worry about losing your job. Everything is confidential." Not only did I lose my job, but I also lost my career.

So, much later—after my wife already left me—I am going to the pet store to buy some fish food. I get in line and who walks up behind me? You guessed it. I gave him a look of absolute disgust and went to the other line. Now I could have publicly humiliated him like he did me by calling him a child abuser, but I turned the other cheek. I was actually on the way to my Baptism.

Another thing I should mention about this guy's character is that when I went to court, my attorney and I were given the allegations much prior—so we could prepare. We were told that I wasn't being charged with anything. This guy...

_____ ..... admittedly slipped the judge different paperwork and I was railroaded to charges I did not commit. It went so fast that I didn't even know what I was admitting. After it was too late, my attorney told me they charged me with "Physical Harm" to my children.

I tried to appeal and was denied. I spoke with a manager at DSS and she said, "I was right there in court when you admitted to it!" My attorney went to bat for me and said their attorney agreed to reduce it to "Threat of Harm." However, when asked for proof that this was done, nobody can give it to me. Do you find that odd? What is the ONLY word that could describe this phenomenon in our (dis)trusted officials? VINDICTIVENESS!!!!!!!!

Chapter 18

The Downside to Using Drugs:

Remember that we should be a county that shouldn't judge or be vindictive, as long a person's actions don't hurt anyone but him or herself. In my case, I believe I was doing drugs recreationally for two reasons. For one, it was self-medicating. It truly balanced me and made me a happy person overall before it turned into a massive addiction. The second reason, I won't lie, is that it was super fun.

However, let me tell you about the crashes. When you use cocaine in any form, after you are done, it brings you down for a while. It makes you feel like crap and depressed. I got used to these crashes and got to a point where I knew what to expect. They weren't fun though. I truly felt it was worth it in my case, but when I crashed, it really did suck.

Even though I believe in legalizing all drugs on isolated geographic grounds, I still believe in educating our kids in the school system to stay away from them. I would encourage anyone never to try drugs. This may sound hypocritical, but it's not. If you do drugs recreationally that is your choice and I will not judge you. I am simply saying that there are some downsides that I would hate for you to have to go through.

Actually, I can honestly say that drugs didn't eat at my bank account because I would only use what I could easily afford. I had a budget. However, if a tragedy strikes that enrages you; if you are dehumanized and destroyed and you have to completely redefine your identity, then that recreational or self-medicated use could turn into a massive addiction. This happened to me because I did so much at once, since I wanted death--I believe it changed my body chemistry.

They say that cocaine can lead to heart complications. A friend told me of a couple people he knew that died from crack cocaine overdoses. However, I am super strong and that kind of thing seems impossible in my case, but people are made differently.

That's all I have to say about cocaine. We know what crystal meth can do by the documentaries and propaganda and that is true. Have you seen the before and after photos? Before using meth people look like people and after several years of massive use they look a little creepy.

I have personally used crystal meth on a recreational level and never got hooked. It was fun, but it did lead to crashes like cocaine. Again, let me reiterate that drugs are your choice and no one should judge you. I'm just throwing in some downsides for your information.

As far as marijuana goes, I was shocked that it wasn't legalized in California at this point in time. However, you simply need to get a prescription and you can legally smoke it in that state. I personally only like marijuana when I'm passing out to a movie. Some downsides for me are that it makes me sleepy and sometimes paranoid. That is why I can't do it socially. I really don't like it that much.

Now, let me tell you the downsides to some legal drugs. We all know what smoking leads to: lung cancer, heart disease...

Did you know that alcohol is the most dangerous drug out there? Once your liver is hardened with cirrhosis, you can never get it back. Alcohol causes more deaths from drinking and driving and to individuals that drink it regularly than any other drug. That sounds so ironic, because it is legal while other drugs are not. The reason is simple: $$$$$$$$$$$$$$$$$

Do you know how much profit businesses would lose, as well as the drop in tax revenue if we returned to Prohibition? Yes it kills people all the time, both bystanders and drinkers, but we keep it legal. Imagine how much money the government would take in if it got all the profits from legalizing every drug in existence. That enactment would truly jettison us into a mega-power financially and help us to afford so many things that other countries can't.

If you are still vindictive toward people who do drugs, you can help legalize all drugs for vindictive reasons. You can think "all those drug 'users' are putting money into the hands of the government and I get to have free world-class health care now; the cities are cleaned up and I have a nice place to live; I'm not taxed as much because the government takes in so much revenue off drug 'users' that there isn't a need; the murder and crime rate have significantly dropped, as well as the spread of HIV."

Truly think about how our deficit could turn into a surplus. Could you imagine our country being out of debt? My ideas would set us on that course.

A huge point I want to bring up that most people don't think about is in regards to alcohol. I am not saying make it illegal, but why is it that 1000's of innocent men, women and children are killed every year by a drunk driver? Alcohol hurts and kills people who aren't even drinking. Why is it that if someone does an illicit substance that only hurts themselves, the government destroys them, when in fact by making alcohol legal the government is actually in an indirect way committing 1000's of murders each year (I am actually working toward being a career bartender—the only reason I bring this up is to make a point)? If you kill someone because you've been drinking too much, then that was the wrong choice to have made and you deserve your punishment.

Also, since alcohol is the worst drug for you, why is it that you can go to a club and it is cool to drink alcohol? Simply that it is the way you are programmed. Crack can actually be glamorized too if money was to be made by corporations. However, I want to make a huge point that even when it does get legalized within certain boundaries, I don't believe it should be advertised to increase government revenue. That would be wrong. Even though alcohol is worse than crack, crack is more addicting and you really shouldn't even try it. Remember though that I will never judge you and as long as you don't hurt anyone but yourself, then it is simply your choice in my opinion. You know the downsides; it's your choice as a human being.

Did you know that in some societies, cocaine leaves were chewed and used as a part of their cultural heritage? Look at the ancient South American Indians. They chewed the coca leaf for thousands of years living and thriving just fine.

Even after the Aztec Emperor Montezuma allowed the Spanish Conquistadors to enter his boundaries of

Tenotchitlon unopposed and was tricked into giving away his riches and then murdered, the Spaniards taxed the indigenous people 10% on coca leaves. The Spaniards made a lot of money doing this. That money further helped to empower Spain.

A country can truly get to zero dollars deficit, have all kinds of funds to spend on bettering the quality of life of its people, and take away the power of its enemies by simply profiting on all drug revenue. Conversely, we are going into debt more and more, fighting the unsinkable drug cartel warship and putting all the profits into the pockets of the dealers, mules, middlemen and drug lords.

Chapter 19

If I Was a Cop or Working for DSS:

I have friends who are cops and work for DSS. I am not against them personally (I still feel that they need to follow the "Universal Declaration of Human Rights"), but to get real, I truly thought about what it would be like having one of these careers. I couldn't even apply. I am such a real person that I truly wouldn't be able to feel good about my job.

I do love what the cops do for this country! They keep us in order and every country needs that. However, if I were required to arrest someone for simple possession I would be heart broken.

I only flipped off a cop one time in my life. It was during my phase of suicidal madness, when I truly lost the will to live. Since I had a clouded judgment, one time on my way to work, I saw two cop cars going the opposite direction. My first gut instinct was to flip them off. When I saw them turn around I quickly tried to hide in my car behind some trees.

They found me and were pissed. I apologized and to this day, I feel bad about that. It's not the cops' fault they have to kidnap kids with DSS. It turned out one of the cops was the same guy who gave me the DUI and he seemed to be the one in charge of the 4 cops that rushed my car. After I apologized, I think he probably felt sorry for me and let me go.   Some cops are corrupt though. Actually, I believe that this particular cop did stretch the truth when he gave me a DUI for "swerving and weaving." However, I can sense that for the most part he is a good guy.

I had a small party at my house last night and I met this guy who told me a story. This guy is very intelligent and he reminds me of roll model students I had when I was teaching. I didn't ask him, but he probably got straight A's.

Anyway, I told him about my book and he told me of a time when the cops busted up a party and he was searched. He had a couple crumbs of marijuana and went to jail. Furthermore, the cops went through his cell phone, and everything he had on him. That was unconstitutional by the way, but it's real.

I told him that for that reason, I could not be a cop. If I believed in the system however, I wouldn't feel hypocritical and would love to be a cop! Being a cop would be so cool because then cops would truly serve a purpose for the good of society.

As it is now, cops go after people who truly don't hurt society in the least bit. They ruin people's lives who, in my opinion didn't even do anything wrong. Could you be a cop? In a perfect system, everyone would love and respect cops because they would truly be there to protect society from the people who hurt other people.

Along the same lines, I could never work for DSS. I have seen first-hand how destroyed children become after being taken from their parents. I would truly feel like a child abuser.

I have some really good advice to ALL cops and people who work for DSS. Turn a blind eye anytime you are forced to destroy someone who didn't hurt anyone but themselves. That would be the right thing to do. Also, leave people alone who don't hurt society.

If you are a cop being videoed by your cruiser camera, then try to base your actions on what can't be seen that you could be held accountable for by the system. That is truly the right thing to do for the good of mankind.

If you work for the SS (DSS), and you get a report that someone may be doing drugs that has kids.

Remember, that is NOT child abuse. It is not worth destroying the family, kidnapping the child and damaging them for life--nor is it worth psychologically damaging the parents and dehumanizing all the victims involved.

Truly follow this advice and base your actions around the "Universal Declaration of Human Rights." One day we will have a utopian society where everyone respects you guys. You guys in a way are victims of the system too because you are forced to commit crimes against humanity when you are just doing your job.

If you can't follow the basic principles of humanity, my advice is that you should get out.

Something else that I wanted to mention in this chapter is about a gal that spent the night on my recliner chair last night from England. This young lady is very interesting because she is African

American with a British accent; she actually sounds just like Kelly Osborn (Ozzie's daughter). Originally she was born in South Africa and gave up her citizenship there to have dual-citizenship between the United States and England. The only reason she did that is that you can't have triple citizenship.

Anyway, I brought up my book as a conversation piece, as we were all sitting around couches enjoying the fire, and she fully connected and related to my ideas. In fact, she affirmed that other countries feel that America is too cocky and pushy, just like I believe. After we connect on Facebook, I am going to get her a copy of my book so she could share it with people in Europe. I am grateful to have met her.

Remember the butterfly effect? Maybe this chance meeting will lead her to give this to a professor or influential person in Europe that will cause an international movement for us to be a better nation. Then, once Congress and the President feel that pressure, we might just become a better nation.

Something else that got brought up at our fireside chat is that in 2001, Portugal decriminalized anyone who possesses any drug. This includes the entire gamut from heroin to marijuana.

I have a message for Portugal: You are before your time and the world will follow your lead. I have the utmost respect for your country. You truly are a real "humanitary" nation. *

There is one more comment I'd like to add in this chapter. Remember the guy I was telling you that was over at my house last night? He was telling me about a friend recently who was as good of a friend as he is with my roommate. He said that someone shot this friend of his in that friend's own house not too long ago over marijuana. I just thought to myself that that guy would still be alive today if we followed Portugal's system of government, but with our own twist.

*The word "humanitary" isn't in the dictionary and is self-invented, but I am still using it because it is the only word that makes perfect sense in the given context.

Chapter 20

My First Blue Christmas:

I have never in my life had a blue Christmas. This is the first year ever, 2010. I have always been used to spending the holidays with family, but I am all alone this year. I wonder why? Seriously though, my roommate went to see his dad in another state, and I am just sitting here by myself. My oldest is also struggling big time and yet she has everyone around but me.

That poor girl is very troubled; it is so sad. If she were just left alone when there wasn't even a problem she still might be full of life. It was horribly cruel what DSS did to her. She was just so full of light and curiosity before. I remember raising her and she had all kinds of questions for me and there was a certain sparkle in her eye. Now, all that faith and stability she had in her dad has been blown to bits by the legal system. I know she can judge for herself, but to the DSS workers: You ruined that poor child and you truly are child abusers.

Anyway, I've actually tried calling my family several times, but they keep-having-to-go because they are "busy"...

My parent's did convince me though to come out with an "edited version." That is smart. People will be more accepting of my "edited version" and then I can come out with the "Director's Cut" once I no longer need an employer. If I came out with my very raw feelings and opinions without holding back, people might not be ready yet (again, I will only come out with that version if I believe that it will truly better mankind). I believe once people see me as a human being and I build a repoire with them that they will be accepting for me to take it to the next level of realness. I feel that it is important, one day, for people to see the raw feelings unedited before they were toned down for the public--again, that might never happen based on my judgment of the benefits outweighing the downsides.

Anyway, getting back to Christmas Eve, I tried calling a bunch of friends to come over, but they are with family. It's December 24th, 11:04 PM Eastern time and I have no one right now. I feel like the man on the moon.

I am actually in so much pain in this one moment I am thinking about doing drugs again because they take the pain away, even it only lasts 5 hours-- depending on the amount I buy. I actually hate being alive right now in this moment (1st Christmas Eve without a family). I'm sure I'll get through without "using" though. (I'm checking back at 2:55 AM and I made it through. I'm starting to actually get tired. Checking in at [this time is after the below time because I just happened to focus on this paragraph at that particular time] 10:48 AM, Dec. 25th—didn't get weak. I'm going to the store to get some cigs instead.)

I just talked to a friend who was telling me about someone he knows that committed suicide. I actually hear lots of these stories but he was telling me that the reason people do it is to get people to feel bad and sorry. I think people kill themselves for lots of reasons, but mine is simply that this world serves me too much pain to even handle being alive at times.

Actually I believe this book is saving me because I have now put hours of time into it without doing drugs. Remember that I have tried to die doing drugs, so no-drugs/no-death. You guys would miss me after reading my book, but that wouldn't be my intent. Actually after talking to my friend that just called, I feel a lot better. Hey, it is now 1:55 AM, Dec. 24th, [I just happened to focus on this paragraph and that is why this time is before the above time] and no drugs!

Now, if I chose to do crack I would still be binging right about now. I might possibly could have run out by 3 or 4:00 AM and then I would experience my crash. Right now though, I could be super high and not feeling any pain. Do you feel my pain? I'm good though.

I'm not going to "use" tonight. I'm just going to go to bed and fall asleep to "Without a Paddle," with Seth Green (Check back at 10:51 AM, Dec 25th—I fell asleep to this movie again without being able to see the end). I am so pissed that I can't find my remote I wrote a rap about it. The problem is that I can't fast-forward on the DVD unit itself. See, I'm distracting myself in other activities, but I have nothing to prove to anyone. Portugal accepts people for who they are and I'm really thinking about moving there and sharing my book with them.

I'm going to get real though. I'm feeling okay now, but earlier I truly wanted to end my life and the last time I did crack-cocaine, I honestly thought I was fading out. I actually dove on my bed because I could feel myself passing out as I was holding in my hit, and I thought that if I lived through it, I could wake up to some broken bones or a disfigured face. Everything started to go dark and I could barely take in any light through my eyes. The problem is that the thought of blowing my brains out with a gun is too scary for even me.

You got to have a lot of respect for people who risk their lives daily in Iraq and Afghanistan, even though I think we need to chill out as a county with going to war. Those soldiers have my complete respect and I appreciate everything they do for our country.

In fact, just the other day I ran into a guy at a karaoke club who was home for the holidays from Afghanistan. He had two Purple Hearts and was a really cool guy. I asked him how many people he's killed so far and he told me that his "*confirmed* kills are currently at 47." I enjoyed hanging out with him. I also asked what it was like to kill somebody and he said that he figures they are going to die anyway, so he's just kind of ending their lives a little early.

I did think to myself that it is a shame that the United States has to kill so many people over what I believe to be the expansion of our power and to increase our oil supply. However, soldiers are the best because they are laying down their lives for our country. DSS workers on the other hand are making a conscious choice to abuse children. I believe they (as well as a lot of America) have been brainwashed in a very cult-like fashion, but a child abuser is a child abuser—brainwashed or not.

Still, there are some good people in that service for all the right reasons. There were also some really good Nazis too who tried to help the Jews. "Schindler's List" was an awesome movie! If you haven't seen it yet, you should definitely check it out.

The state of affairs with the legal-system abusing children is such a sad and pitiful situation. I am actually starting to feel sorry for the government because if they aren't doing it for vindictive reasons they may just be too stupid. However, I don't put it past them to simply not care, because their financial interests are more important to them than abusing people.

Getting back to the soldier with the two Purple Hearts: my friend's brother actually has Post Traumatic Stress Disorder from doing the same thing overseas. He is damaged for life. Some people can handle seeing their friend's head blown off, along with mass killings of the enemy, and other people get damaged for life.

I believe that when you get your children taken, after talking with many victims—both children I taught and parents—some people get Post Traumatic Stress Disorder and others don't. It's so sad that the legal system hasn't done their research and don't seem to care about ruining lives. If the legal system is giving children PTSD for life when the child otherwise would have a happy upbringing, that simply equates to abuse. The legal system abuses children—it is my belief that the shear amount of children they abuse and indirectly murder (through foster neglect) far outreaches the tiny numbers of actual child abuse that really occurs.

At the end of World War 2, the Cold War began. There was a movement in this country that made everyone paranoid about thinking people were Communists. This guy Joe MacCarthy started this movement in 1950 that would later be called the "Communist Witch Hunt." I believe there is a similar movement in America today that I call the Child Abuser Witch Hunt. Most the people the government went after back then weren't even Communists and yet their lives were destroyed. Ask yourself, could the government be wrong again?

Something else I have noticed is a pattern in people. Most people want to hear me out thinking I am just venting but then they tell me I need to move on and just focus on the future. Well, for me, this is my way of moving on. I am doing what I believe to be right.

What if you guys didn't have me around? What if Galileo never existed? Talk about injustice, he figured out that the solar system revolves around the sun and not the earth. Do you realize how much flack he caught? It was absolutely torturous for him. He was simply before his time.

I was thinking I might be the only person like this, but after I connected with that girl from England last night I now believe people's philosophical thought pattern in significantly influenced for most people by their country. If I were given the power of God, like in the movie "Bruce Almighty," that would be the best ever (if he gave me permission to reign as *I will*). I would help save 10's of thousands from whatever horrible injustice the legal system is bestowing upon them.

Now that I think about it though, a lot of people agree with me. In fact, that is why I got kicked out of one particular (DSS-mandated) drug rehab center. People in my classes were getting too fired up about my ideas and instead of the focus being on handling addiction it kept turning into a DSS bashing. This one class instructor finally just didn't want me there anymore and started a movement to get rid of me. I was just telling how I felt though and wasn't intentionally trying to take away from his leadership.

At first, any new thinker is sloughed off and/or rejected. In fact people get tired of them and say, "Hey look, we just don't see the benefit of your ideas. You're crazy!" Let me ask you this, what if there weren't people like me in the world? Crucial change would never occur. I am here to help--always remember that.

Getting back to my first blue Christmas. Like I said, I am actually thinking about moving to Portugal and disappearing off the map. That would be pretty cool, but I would always want to keep in contact with my kids. That is the problem. What a dilemma. I would love though to share my story with the people of Portugal. I could probably be fully open with them and not have to worry about not being able to work again.

I am actually writing right now because the computer is the only thing that will be there for me. I'm actually a really cool guy and I don't want to sound desperate, but imagine losing your family and being isolated 3,000 miles away from where you lived most your life. This is definitely a rough day for me. Honestly though, I don't believe I am capable of suicide other than death-by-overdose, so there is really nothing to worry about. It'll be cool. I can keep myself clean.

I am just really lonely and hate it at this particular given moment. I need to find a girlfriend maybe. I've been putting the ladies off telling them that I'm not ready for a relationship. Keep in mind that I have been through a lot and I didn't need a girlfriend before I was married.

Maybe that is my solution. I feel weird about it because I am still technically married, but a girlfriend who could actually be there for me in my time of need may help me cope with reality.

I have actually met some pretty badass women lately. This one girl has tats (tattoos) all over her body that are all very-well-thought-out and meaningful. She wears rattlesnake-skin hats, stilettos and is hardcore into 80's rock. That's my kind of girl! I just feel like I can relate because I'm a badass guy, in a cool sense—I am tatless (without tattoos) at this time however.

On the other hand, she has a boyfriend who plays in a pretty big band (she is very loyal to him); I totally respect that (it's not like I like her in that way anyway—I mean…yeah, whatever). I actually just like hanging out with her and doing karaoke—karaoke night is the highlight of my week; I get crazy on the microphone because I have too. I do cool rap hits and get the place rockin'.

Getting back to the dating situation, I'm stuck now because I love my wife, but don't know if she'll ever come home, and man it is lonely in that regard. I have a roommate and we have people over, but I miss having someone to come home to that loves me.   My conscience is telling me to just keep my friendships with the ladies on a purely platonic level—actually I really don't feel ready yet. Besides, the ladies I work with are all very pretty, but most of them are too young for me. The ones who are not have boyfriends or even if they are single, like I said, "I'm not ready for a relationship."

So if my divorce becomes final, where can I find my dream girl? Maybe I should try Match.com? This so sounds like a plug, like this company is paying me to say that, but in reality I am a nobody at this point in my life. One day though, I may have it all again. I just need to take it one day at a time and rebuild the life that the legal system destroyed.

What would I do if I had it all again? Honestly, if I make enough money I really might just move to Portugal with my next wife. I truly thought my first wife would be there forever, but most women are completely loyal to their government over their husbands—even when the government is wrong.

Don't get me wrong, I am completely loyal too, but I also think the government is made up of elite people who take advantage of their power and are inhumane to the people they represent sometimes. I love Thomas Jefferson! I hate DSS. I love Barack Obama! I hate our inhumane laws.

Getting back to moving to Portugal with my future next wife. I wouldn't do it for the drugs (since all drugs are legal); I would do it because I would feel a

part of a humane society that accepts me for me and everyone else for who they are. That, my friends, is a utopian society. In a "humanitary" sense, I believe they are the most progressive country in the world. *
I don't know much else about them, but so far I am hearing of great strides they have made toward humanizing everyone.

Wow! It's hard to imagine a country without any inhumane laws. See, it can be done! It's a shame that the United States didn't do it first. Portugal is putting us to shame. We are truly getting behind the times and letting other nations pass us. One day, we will be miniscule in the overall scheme of the world because some of our international leaders are pretty dumb.

I just feel like Portugal is probably the best place in the world to raise a family because they are a country that doesn't have inhumane laws that I am aware of at this time. If you believe your country is doing wrong and you can't change them, you have the choice to go to a government that doesn't abuse people.

By the way, guess how many gifts I got this year? I received one from a coworker because we did a secret Santa (drawing a name out of a hat and buying them a gift). My mom got me something as well and my oldest daughter sent me a handmade card with her picture: "Dear Dad, how are you doing. I love you very much you're my Best Dad. Love you By. Love, _____."

When it is found out that you do or did drugs, your loved ones turn on you. Not all of them, but enough for you to feel major repercussions. I'm not trying to feel sorry for myself or get you to feel sorry for me; I am just being real.

*Again, the word "humanitary" isn't in the dictionary and is self-invented, but I am still using it because it is the only word that makes perfect sense in the given context.

Chapter 21

It's a Nation-Wide Epidemic:

Something I just thought about right now--because the California Department of Social Services is trying to collect child support from me--is what they put me through. This particular incident has nothing to do with drugs.

Let's roll back the clock to 2002 when my first daughter was born. I had been telling my wife and her best friend NOT to put my daughter on the couch or bed because my protective instincts would go crazy. I didn't think it was safe. They kept calling me a "worrywart" and my wife's best friend kept saying, "It's okay, I let my kids on the couch and bed when they were babies."

So one day, I was asleep on the bed. My wife placed our baby beside me without my awareness whatsoever. I woke up to a thud and our baby crying. I was devastated and so worried about my daughter that I rushed her to the emergency room.

So Social Services comes into the picture, comes in my house and starts antagonizing me. They start pushing me with their vindictive attitude. They tell me that I am to get rid of my cats and so on. They actually left my wife alone completely. My teaching credential got put on hold for 3 months as a result.

Then, I had to take my daughter to get a series of tests down in the basement of this hospital. I call it the dungeon because I believe it only exists for the SS (DSS) cases. Anyway there was a father who was upset with the staff. He was very enraged in fact. They kept pushing and pushing him even though he was most likely a victim, as most parents I know are. When he left, they laughed and said, "The only reason he is so mad is because he is a child abuser."

So I check in and they must have put my daughter through $50,000 or more worth of tests; it took at least 4 or 5 hours. They x-rayed her feet and hands in one room, a cat scan of some sort in another, a doctor looked into her retina in another with a blinding light; we were moved from room to room to room. It went on and on. Meanwhile I was treated like a "child abuser."

At the end of it all I went to the supervisor's room holding my daughter on my lap. The lady looked me dead in the eye and said, "Sorry. It turns out that we might have made a mistake." I was so pissed I wanted to slap her even though I would never lay a hand on a woman. Ask yourself this though: Was it about the money they made from the tests, or was it really about finding a "child abuser?"

Again, the problem with our legal system is we push and push people to have ill feelings toward it. Did you know that the word "Pig" (a derogatory name for a cop) would never exist if all the laws focused on protecting society instead of finding inhumane ways for the government to increase profits?

Who hates Portugal? Since all drugs are legal there and they have very humane laws—not to mention they don't push people in other nations—they are a perfect society. You'd probably expect their crime rate to be high but it is low. In fact, since they have legalized drugs, they have seen a mass decrease in death rate by overdose and spread of HIV.

Interesting how I foresaw that before I even knew Portugal decriminalized drugs. So am I really crazy or do I have the perfect solution? Really search in your hearts to find the answer. We could be the best nation in the world if we really wanted.

Chapter 22

The Second Time I almost Went to Jail:

This one time, I called up one of my middlemen. I am going to significantly limit details on this one because he went to jail for a long time and is still battling the legal system. This guy has one of the best characters on the face of the planet. He loves his mom and his mom loves him back dearly. He is one of the nicest guys I have ever met.

Anyway, I met him and drove him to a spot by a dealer's house when the rest of my connections didn't come through. I gave him the money like I usually did and waited. After over an hour I left baffled because this guy wasn't like that. Something wasn't right.

I called his mom and his mom got really worried. I called his brother and his brother hadn't seen him. After 3 months went by, I was meeting a dealer about 15 miles away from where this took place. Suddenly this guy who I first mentioned comes out of nowhere and wants to get in my car. My dealers are very protective of me and my dealer was ready to fight this guy.

This guy kept telling me to tell my dealer that I know him so my dealer would back off. I did. So I'm driving away with this guy and I said, "Dude, what happened that day?" He said, "Man it was a set up. Cops stormed in and I got put in jail for 3 months." I told him that I was so sorry and still was a little suspicious, but you know how you can just tell if someone went through some serious stuff and isn't lying? I just kept listening to the details of his lawyer, who I know personally, as well as about when he was in jail.

Man, this guy lives with his mom and is a very nice and caring person. He wouldn't hurt a soul. That was so not cool of the legal system. I personally believe he didn't do a thing wrong because who did he hurt? Who did the legal system have to protect him from?

I told him about the "butterfly effect" and that if I hadn't called him that day on that hour, he may never have gone to that house that was awaiting the next buyer. He definitely agreed with me and promised to watch "The Butterfly Effect," with Ashton Kutcher. To this day, I feel really bad, but you know what? Rule number one of the streets: Never snitch.

I asked him about that though because I'm not the type of guy to go shoot someone over snitching. He made sure I didn't go down with him because he knew I would have done the same for him. It was the right thing to do.

Was it really necessary to send this guy to jail for buying drugs? No way! He is one of the most kind, gentle and "humanitary" African-Americans that has ever lived. He is all about peace and loves his mom and family dearly. Again, who did sending this guy to jail protect? The answer is simple. It didn't protect a single person. It just ruined this guy's life for no justified reason. The fact that our legal system causes more harm than good is just so sad.

The reason I put this chapter at the end is hopefully by now you lost your vindictive attitude toward people who do drugs. I am doing everything I can to humanize them back to life--kind of like the African-American kids in my class who used to always ask me why all the Presidents have been white; then we elected Barack Obama. These kids were humanized over night.

That is what it will be like when we make all drugs legal like Portugal has done. Kids, parents, cousins, friends and so on of anybody who is in jail for simple possession will break down crying because the pain

is finally over, but the scar will forever remain.

*Again, the word "humanitary" isn't in the dictionary and is
self-invented, but I am still using it because it is the only word
that makes perfect sense in the given context.

Chapter 23

A Live Chat with a DSS Employee:

"Hey, I hope you had a Merry Christmas!"

"Hey, I wrote a book. I put that I have friends in the SS (DSS), but common? In a year or two the DSS system will catch a lot of flack, but I'm trying to protect my friends. Merry Christmas! I am probably going to be on a national talk show within the next year or two. I am on a mission to save the children. If you'd like, I will give you a copy after my editor is done. Again, you are protected."

"Really? I would like a copy. Who is publishing it?"

"Actually I know what I want and that's what I'm going to get. I will give you a copy of the edited version.

The "Director's Cut" will come out at a much later date."

"Lol. Ok. I thought fourth grade took a great loss when you left teaching."

"DSS simply causes more harm than good, but we could agree to disagree. You need to read the book detailing the 100% real stories from the parents, children and so much more…"

"There are good things and bad things…"

"I didn't get out of fourth grade, DSS pushed me out."

"I know and it was a shame. I was surprised that the school could do that with DSS info. I'm tired of the way things are going in protective services. I feel like I am the only one who cares!!!"

"Maybe if you read the book, you could add some real-life stories from the inside, but that is up to you. I am truly a humanitarian and I believe I am doing the right thing for the children."

"I think there are lot's of things done there that should not be…some things are really slack, while others are just insane, insane, and sick. I can't take it any more!"

"Children are suffering from being removed from their biological parents. The ACLU agrees with me. I have included the letters in my book. I can't do my book justice by chatting. I will get you a copy when it is ready."

"OK. Well…I am always here. I will say also that some of the judges I have been in with think they are high and mighty too. They don't relate well with common people."

"Thanks. Always do what you think is best for the children, even if the legal system doesn't know better. One day we will have a utopian society. My book is called 'Injustice for All Ages.'"

"Good title." *End of conversation*

Final Thoughts:

How many people over the ages were hurt by our selfish, "inhumanitary" and greedy ways? * This book is also dedicated to the Native Americans (who were slaughtered and forced off their land), the Irish (during the time of the transcontinental railroad), black people--the most (slavery, segregation…), women who weren't allowed to vote, the inmates at Abu Ghraib, the innocent women and children who die when we fire missiles sometimes at targeted buildings, the victims of the South Carolina perp paper, the people during the 1950's who were falsely dubbed Communists, the people who served time or had Capital Punishment when they were innocent, the inmates in jail for life or awaiting Capital Punishment because they defended themselves from being raped, the supposed Salem witches, the Latinos (currently being used as cheap labor in California), the Japanese victims annihilated by our nukes (or left with cancer), the Japanese people who were victimized at US internment camps during WW II, the victims of foreclosure criminally caused by the home loan industry (*houses of broken dreams*), the victims of corrupt corporations (Enron, Adelphia Cable, Worldcom...), the innocent victims of gang shootouts that should still be alive, the murder victims of the drug cartels, the drug addicts that contracted and spread HIV because they needed their next fix and couldn't legally get help (performing sexual favors), all those who had their culture stripped from them during any given deculturalization process, the soldiers that died during unjustified wars (and their families), the children that are inhumanely taken from their parents and left broken (and their families)...

The only justice I will probably receive is when I file bankruptcy and make the legal-system pay for the harm they caused to my family. I actually would otherwise want to pay back every cent on my own. Call it my lawsuit, but I really feel entitled to more than a million dollars and even that wouldn't be enough to give me real justice.

Did you know that when our founding fathers put together our Constitution they felt hypocritical, but they needed something to get our new country in order? Don't get me wrong, I love our Constitution; I love our country; I love most of our laws and feel they are needed; I love Hollywood movies; I love the NFL as well as college football; I love just about everything about my country, but we need to simply do away or significantly limit the injustices: *It's time for a utopian society*.

I also want to say that I believe my ideas are the *best-in-the-world* and the right means to solving the majority of injustice in our country (not to mention an ongoing significant reduction of our national deficit, job creation, having a real face around the world that other countries respect, promoting world-wide peace, significantly reducing the tension between the US People and its legal system…). Eventually, when my vision becomes a reality, I promise nothing but the sweet taste of pure victory and justice for all. However, I am just here to help guide other leaders. Don't expect me to run for office because after doing some soul searching I have realized that is not what I want.

By the way, do you know how they determine the building of future prisons? They base their plans around third grade literacy scores. Why? They know that these kids will most likely not be able to get good jobs and resort to dealing drugs. It's that simple.

Another comment I'd like to add is regarding the police. Did you know that they have a certain quota to meet as far as traffic tickets, DUI's, and so on? The law enforcement is run like a business and officers get bonuses based on how many people they catch doing whatever. The reason for this is simple: $$$$$$$$$$$$$$$$$$$$$$$$$$$$$$$$$$$$$$ That is why some people are profiled leaving clubs or bars, even if they only had a couple beers and had time to sober up. The city simply could use the money, whether people are innocent or not. Have you ever thought how they got all the funding to build the fancy justice buildings?

Instead of being money hungry, the police need to truly get back to having integrity and serving in the

public's best interest in all cases. Police bonuses
based on quotas needs to be eliminated.

Again, there needs to be another Revolution.
Hopefully we can have this Revolution without
bloodshed. The problem is that we have a system
that is almost impossible to change democratically.
So what do we do as a country, keep-on tolerating
the human rights violations of our legal system
against its people? You answer that for yourself.

I truly believe deep down in my heart that my vision
for the future of America would *definitely* get the
stamp of approval from Thomas Jefferson.
Absolutely! Why? My ultimate solution simply solves
the majority of our nations problems. Again, I am 50
to 500 years from the future; at least that is how I
feel. One day my ideas will become America's
reality, so why not end the problems now?

"Every new generation needs a Revolution."

Thomas Jefferson

I want to finish this section of my book on a positive note. A while back, a daughter of a female friend of mine fell while playing and hit her head on a coffee table. My friend and the child's dad acted as any caring parent would and immediately took the child to the hospital. I got wind of this and counseled the mom *immediately*. I told her my story, and prepped her on what was to come.

I told her that DSS was going to come into the picture and drug test both her and the father. I also told her that she needed to have a relative lined up to prevent the child from going into foster care and being psychologically destroyed for the rest of her life.

This friend of mine followed my advice and when the time came to remove the child, she was placed with a caring relative. I helped save that child and I want to help save millions more.

Now, on a more serious note: Are we really
discouraging parents from seeking the proper
medical care for their child in need? The answer
to that is YES. Absolutely!

By the way, this situation caused the break-up of
the mother and father's relationship, which didn't
surprise me.

*The word "inhumanitary" isn't in the dictionary and is self-
invented, but I am still using it because it is the only word
that makes perfect sense in the given context.

A Message to ANYONE Who Is Pushed to the Brink and Is Plotting a War-Style Counter-Attack:

Trust me, I've been there. I know what you are feeling and going through. You may be the victim of being bullied at your school. You may be a victim of a heinous crime. You may have been victimized by the people you are supposed to trust the most.

I called my good friend in California who I have known since childhood. When we were about 5 years old, he was the first person I was taught to trust as a concept. What I mean by that is I didn't know what trust meant, but our camp counselor took us to a sacred spot in the woods. He blindfolded me and then, as I was standing, he told me to fall back and my friend would catch me. I then caught my friend. I am now 35 years old and this memory has formed a bond between my friend and me forever.

When times are tough, your fake friends will run and hide. They won't return your calls. They may fear guilt by association. This particular friend on the other hand was there for me. If you are going through a lot, find that friend. Maybe he or she wasn't bonded to you when you first learned about trust, but most people have a good heart and someone will understand your situation. There are also thousands of really good psychologists out there that will help you better understand your feelings of rage and how to express them in a healthy manner. Killing people will only turn you from victim to a condemned assailant.

This friend I am talking about told me a story. His friend happens to be a trusted cop—proof that anyone is capable of that psychological edge that can cause ANYONE to snap. He received a call that his daughter was raped. He happened to know the guy and drove right to his house with a baseball bat. His first objective was to murder the rapist. Right before the police arrived; right before he took out his slew of vengeance; he got a phone call from one of his TRUE friends. That friend helped him to see the repercussions of his actions that he could not see himself because his judgment was clouded. This man put down his bat and the rapist was brought to justice when the cops arrived.

I have another story that demonstrates what I call the "Psychological Brink Phenomenon" that turns a victim into a perpetrator. When I was PE Coach out at a school in the San Fernando Valley, California, I was engaging the children in a game of dodge ball. Some bullies kept picking on this one kid. This kid started breathing heavy and was at the point of snapping.

I pulled him aside and explained to him that he is a victim and that I was so sorry he had to go through that. I assured him that I would send the bullies in for counseling and reprimand. I told him that if he reacted the way he truly wanted, then he would no longer be a victim; he would then be the one in trouble.

As I was taking the bullies in, they taunted him one last time. This kid then ran up to one of the bullies that was out of my reach and socked him square in the nose. Blood gushed everywhere. This kid then went from victim to getting suspended for 5 days.

What is my point? Knowledge is power. When you are in a time of need like I am right now, write down your thoughts. Fight your enemies with a pen, not your AK-47 assault rifle. However, I still do believe in self-defense and then you have to do what you have to do, just try not to kill them.

So what do you do when the trusted people in charge don't give you the justice you desperately need? What do you do when the law betrays you and commits a crime against humanity? You write. Write your ideas down and get them out there. Put your perpetrators on blast like I have done.

You may ask me if I believe in war. No I don't. However, if there is military aggression that is completely unwarranted like in the bombing of Pearl Harbor, then yes I do. If there is domestic aggression against your human rights, then absolutely! This is my war, fought with Microsoft Word instead of a 9-millimeter handgun.

Be like Martin Luther King Jr. Look at what he accomplished for civil rights. He believed in nonviolent protests, even though the protesters would sometimes be faced with riot gear, tear gas, fire hoses....

Look at what he achieved. His dream did come true partially, but there is still along way to go to obtain a perfect society where "all men are treated equal under the eyes of God."

My second favorite quote of all time is, "Give me liberty or give me death," coined by Patrick Henry. My placement of this quote in this chapter may seem like a paradox. By the way, this is the only time I have ever used the word "paradox" in the right context. I am using it in a sincere, well-thought-out and meaningful way. Think about what it means to you juxtaposed next to my belief that Martin Luther King Jr.'s idea of nonviolent protests are the way to go. I don't mean to sound vague or ambiguous; just interpret this paragraph in your own way.

A message to the people of the future: we will try peacefully as a society to make America a just place to live for everyone, where all men, women and children are given equal opportunities to succeed, as well as, treated according to the "Universal Declaration of Human Rights." However, if enough time has gone by after my death and injustice is still rampant, it is then *necessary* to do whatever it takes to make it right, in the name of humanity.

Never resort to terror though, but it is ok to openly declare another Revolutionary War if Congress is made up of elite people that won't listen to your grievances. Use propaganda and whatever you can to help the majority of the citizens see that they are being horribly wronged. By that time there may be other types of injustices being committed as our rights are diminishing every day. Remember, if it has only gotten worse since my existence and you don't stand up for what you believe in, think of what your children and grandchildren may have to face.

Something Just Came Up:

I know that my book has already ended, but a current event just caught my attention. I can't help myself and need to comment on the "Wiki Leaks" that just came out and embarrassed our government internationally. At this time, Hillary Clinton (Secretary of State) is actively out and about apologizing her tail off to help us save face.

What am I talking about? If you followed the story, the "Wiki Leaks" brought a lot of our government's secretive Intel to light. The part that embarrassed us the most is our arrogance to judge the character of multiple world leaders. Why are we sending out spies and gathering all this secretive Intel, yet at the same time pretending we are completely fine with certain world leaders? We are simply two-faced. We are also insecure because we know a lot of what we do isn't right.

My solution is to get real with other countries. If we feel a certain way, then let them know the truth. Part of our problem getting respect throughout the world is that we don't communicate our feelings and we lie. Then, when lies turn to truth we get embarrassed?

I believe the American people deserve a government that is REAL both domestically and abroad. In addition, I believe that the American people deserve a government that respects the differences between governments and doesn't have the absolute arrogance that our way needs to be followed by the rest of the world.

Think about this: We create hatred against us by our pushy, invasive and judgmental ways. We are also only a nation of 300 to 400 million people. How many people does China have?

They have over 1 billion, probably closer to 2. Did you know that they have the technology to take out satellites with missiles launched from the ground? Did you know that our claim as one of the leading international powers since World War II is slowly dwindling? Did you also know that most of our international defense technology depends on those satellites? Now, how many Middle Easterners are there? Do the math.

It truly wouldn't be that hard, if we acquired enough enemies, for them to plan a massive attack that took out the U.S.A. in one bloody day. I'm not going to get into how it can be done because I don't want to give our enemies any ideas, but just think about that.

The time has come to rebuild America. I also want to reiterate how much I love my country. I am NOT a terrorist. I am simply a humanitarian that cares about human beings that are victims of injustice.

Also, keep this in mind: The government should fear the people, not the reverse. Furthermore, to win a war you need to fear *nothing,* and outsmart your enemy. The legal system is the enemy to many victims. Fight the legal system legally with the power of the written word and propaganda.

I do have one more parting thought; the government *technically* works for the "People" and is by the "People." I use the word "*technically*" in a facetious sense because that statement is so far from reality, and yet it is what we are brainwashed into believing since elementary school. Yes we have elections, but get real. What Democrat or Republican, once voted in, really makes the changes necessary?

I truly believe the only peaceful solution to the harm the legal system is causing both domestically and abroad is to get everybody on the same page and pressure the government. Make the government fear us. Guess what the only downside is? The media isn't objective. The media will possibly try to destroy me and control your feelings, but remember that only *you* are the ultimate judge.

If I end up being too influential for the government or certain radical citizens to handle, I will probably be assassinated—that's if my book takes off. That will only make me a martyr. Nothing will stop my ideas; my death will only make my ideas stronger.

In closing, just remember that the reason the media manipulates your feelings is to control you. Do you truly think the government is afraid of the "People?" No way! The government will never fear us like they should until we unite as one. We can also never unite as one until the majority sees through the media or the media joins our cause: the fight for human rights and against "inhumanitary" oppression. *

*Again, the word "inhumanitary" isn't in the dictionary and is self-invented, but I am still using it because it is the only word that makes perfect sense in the given context.

The House of Broken Dreams:

Have you ever driven through the projects and seen dilapidated housing?

Have you ever seen a house in a decent neighborhood that is no longer lived in and falling apart? Have you ever wondered…could it be…. a house of broken dreams?

There is definitely a story behind that house. You step in the house as the splintery door barley hanging from its hinges creeks open. Under blankets of dust like you'd see in a vacuum bag, you come across an old stained mattress with rusty springs poking through the fabric. Who slept here when the mattress was new? You lift the mattress and cough a couple times on the dust cloud. Beneath the mattress you find a faded dusty picture. You take in a breath and blow on it to get off the dust. You then brush it with your thumb to see the faces. Who were these people?

You see a happy husband and wife and two beautiful girls. Who are they? Are they still a tight-knit family and as happy as they are in the photo? Are they still alive? Did they die in that house (metaphorically)? Are they okay psychologically? What's their story?

You walk outside and something catches your peripheral. You look at the cracked kitchen window and see a reflection of the sun going down. You adjust your vision to see behind the sunset and you notice the ghost of a wife washing dishes.

You look into the overgrown backyard and gaze upon an illusion of a father showing one of his daughters how to ride a bike. She is full of bright light like the sun at midnoon. As she is laughing, smiling and pedaling, her father claps his hands and says, "You did it! I am so proud of you."

Suddenly:

Cop cars,

Children screaming,
Wife crying,

Dad numb,

Who's abusing who?

Kidnapping,

Psychological damage,

Darkness begins,

Post Traumatic Stress Disorder,

Crimes against humanity,

Bright future changing,

The butterfly effect occurring,

"Daddy, daddy, daddy…. Don't let them take me!!!!!!!"

"Daddy!!!"

Social Services leaving,

Neighbors staring,

No contact allowed,

No information given,

Broken promises,

Mom and dad are dying,

Split!

WELCOME TO THE HOUSE OF BROKEN DREAMS

The Final Chapter,

The Divergent Learner:

When I got my Master's Degree in Education, one of the focuses was on the divergent learner. What is the divergent learner? A divergent learner is anyone in the school system that does anything they can to hurt their own education, possibly the education of others, as well as, them being rebellious against authority. By the way, I will submit research articles upon request, but it truly is a common sense concept.

How many divergent learners are there? I found that at least 75% of my students fell into that category. My study can't be generalized however, because it was only a small sampling. On the other hand, that is beside the point.

If the teacher is authoritarian, publicly humiliates, forces the child's education and so on, the divergent learner will resist. The only way to motivate some of these divergent learners is to show you genuinely care and connect with the child. That child can then become a genius.

You may say this sounds like me (the author). A big point I am trying to make is that if our legal-system followed my advice, there wouldn't be these types of ill reactions both domestically and abroad. My reaction on the other hand was very complex. It was divergent based, possibly Post Traumatic Stress Disorder, as well as losing the will to live.

I mastered this psychological phenomenon toward the end of my teaching career. The theme in my class was, "I care. Do you?" I wore an "I Care" button and the students each had "We Care" buttons. I also did everything I could to connect with each and every one of them. These kids, who previously didn't care and weren't motivated, were happy and wanted to learn. If their motivation wasn't for anything else, it was that they wanted to do it for me.

The reason I am bringing this phenomenon up is that the divergent learner concept can simply be applied to all interactions in life. If employers treated their employees in a caring and humanistic fashion, as well as did everything they could to genuinely connect with them (without being a pushover), employees would be more productive and their quality of work would increase. It would be good for business and morale. However, this concept doesn't apply if the employer is fake because the employees would be able to see right through them. You have to be real. I'm not telling business owners how to run their business; I am merely trying to show them how they can easily increase profits.

I also believe that if the legal system showed the same level of caring and tried to connect to all the citizens, we would have less crime. Furthermore, imagine if we applied this concept to our international relations with other countries.

Here is what our leaders need to say, "We respect you and your background. We believe democracy to be the best system in the world and we will help you if you want. However, we appreciate the diversity your system of government brings to the world and want to be neutral in our coexistence." Again, we need to be real. If countries thought we were being real before, the "Wiki Leaks" certainly destroyed that belief.

Remember, I am an expert on the divergent learner concept. I have conducted research on my students (with parental permission) and I have read many research articles. I have also (after synthesizing the information, reflecting on my own teaching practices, and finding truth) given many presentations as a requirement of the Master's program. Moreover, I have applied theory into practice in the classroom and it worked!

Politicians a lot of times are great public speakers, but advisors like me are really needed to help guide their actions and write their speeches.

Parting Thoughts:

In the "Dedication" I thanked the music industry for helping me to express myself as I wrote this book. As a final note, please listen to Michael Jackson's song "Will You Be There?" Conversely, listen to Metallica's "Some Kind of Monster." Don't focus so much on the lyrics--just feel the music (although many of the lyrics are exactly how I feel). The only reason I don't want you to focus so much on the lyrics is that I have not fully analyzed their meaning and don't want to be misinterpreted. In addition, please listen to each song in its entirety. Enough said…

Also, I want to send a BIG shout out to U2 for being the most humanitarian band that ever existed. Bono (and the rest of the band), thanks for what you do. Your music will have a butterfly effect that will help guide the future of the world.

There is just more thing that I need to say. Some people may say that I am "out of touch with reality and need help." This is what one particular family member told me, even though I have been getting a lot of positive feedback from people in various locations throughout the world who agree with me. This particular family member also told me that I needed to erase any existence of my book and get rid of it for good. That's ok. Galileo felt the same level of skepticism. Along the same lines, what if I'm actually right?

Also, what if I didn't speak up? It is absolutely critical that I give victims of the system a voice because if not for me, who would?

Good-bye friends. Always stand up for what you believe in. Always do what you believe to be the best benefit for humanity.